VITAL SIGNS

A MISSION OF THE HEART

VITAL SIGNS

A MISSION OF THE HEART

by Janet Bergera

Covenant Communications, Inc.

Published by Covenant Communications, Inc.
American Fork, Utah

Printed in the United States of America
First Printing: March 1995

95 96 97 98 99 00 01 02 10 9 8 7 6 5 4 3 2 1
ISBN 1-55503-777-1

Chapter One

"Code Blue in ER!" The voice crackled across the PBX system, filling the halls of Mercy Hospital in New York City with its chilling cry. "Code Blue in ER!"

In her three years there as a nurse, and three years before that as a student, those unexpected words never failed to make Julie Craig's heart drop. Springing to her feet, she didn't pause to wonder who was knocking on death's door. She was trained to respond, to act, to save lives.

Halfway across the empty locker room, Julie caught a glimpse of silk and pearls instead of the usual green hospital scrubs in a passing mirror. *Wait a minute,* she thought with a smile. She wasn't on duty. She had merely stopped there on her way to the airport to clean out her locker.

Leave the resuscitation efforts to those on the payroll, she told herself, turning back to the task at hand. It was Easter Sunday, and the emergency room was probably busy. But she had a plane to catch, didn't she?

Julie reached down and scooped up a handful of litter from the bottom of the locker. Before she could drop it into the trash, her surroundings were suddenly plunged into total darkness. *What in the world?!*

Perplexed, Julie stumbled through the inky blackness with her hands stretched out in front of her. Several moments—and bumps on her shins—later, she reached the locker room door. She slipped out into the hall, which was shrouded in shadows.

The lights must be out all over the hospital, she decided as she saw puzzled employees wandering out from every direction. In muted tones, everyone wondered aloud about what had happened. Another urgent message on the intercom answered them. "Attention all units, Code D-2, twenty-five, Code D-2, twenty-five."

Julie's heart dropped again. The call of "Code D-2" meant an external disaster, which could be anything from a gang riot to a terrorist attack to an earthquake. "Twenty-five" indicated the number of victims involved. Things were going to start hopping, especially without electricity.

Curiosity as well as concern propelled Julie toward the emergency center down the hall. Sirens began to wail in the distance as Julie reached the main desk. Suddenly, a dim light flickered overhead. *Emergency generator,* Julie thought as it slowly grew steady, casting a bluish light over the temporary command post.

"Hey, folks," a redheaded nurse called out, drawing Julie's attention away from the lack of lighting. "Welcome to our wonderful world of trauma. A tour bus crashed into a delivery truck nearby. Unfortunately, it took out our power lines in the process. We have at least twenty-five passengers en route to us."

Amidst a round of groans, she threw out assignments with authority. "Johnson, free up some of our rooms if you can. Wright, go out and triage the incoming with Tribbett. Everyone else, heads up. Don't waste time on patients who can wait. Here comes our first customer. Let's go!"

Everyone sprang into action at once. Julie didn't worry that she wasn't officially on duty. When the charge nurse was finished giving instructions, Julie caught her arm. "Can you use another hand, Fern?"

"I wouldn't turn it down," the redhead replied quickly over her shoulder as she directed a stretcher into a nearby room. "Get a lab coat and help out in the south hall."

Julie's assigned area was littered with stretchers and patients. Each had a priority tag attached to the foot of their bed, placed there by triage nurses who quickly assessed their wounds to ensure that the most critically ill were treated first. Priority-one tags indicated life-threatening injuries, while hysterics and abrasions prevailed among priority-four patients.

As Julie reached for a stethoscope, an elderly man with thinning white hair caught her arm. "Hey, little pixie, hold on a minute."

With that, he had her attention immediately. Her father had always called her a pixie. Maybe it was her brown hair or tanned complexion. Perhaps it was her chocolate brown eyes, encircled by dark, thick lashes, or her round lips. Or perhaps it was the sprinkling of freckles upon her upturned nose. At any rate, she smiled. "What can I do for you?"

"I don't feel so good."

"Of course, you don't." Julie studied his tag: priority-three with a broken ankle, a deep laceration on his shoulder, and bruising across his stomach and chest. His wounds needed attention, but none urgently. "You're pretty banged up. Where does it hurt the most?"

The man tapped on his chest. "Here. I can't catch my breath."

"Are you visiting New York?" she asked to distract him while she took his blood pressure. It was low. She listened to his heart as well and found the beats rapid and irregular.

"It's my granddaughter's birthday today." His voice was raspy. "She's eight years old, and they're having a big party. They're expecting me. . . ."

Suddenly, he sat upright, grasped his chest, then fell back with his head rolling flaccidly to one side. Julie frantically tried to arouse him. Nothing. *No,* she wanted to cry out. *No! This grandpa can't die, not on Easter Sunday, not on his granddaughter's eighth birthday!*

She felt a rush of adrenaline as she flattened the stretcher, then tipped the man's head back to open his airway. She checked for signs of breathing. When she found none, she quickly grabbed a mask from a nearby cart and placed it over his mouth, blowing two quick breaths into the mouthpiece. His chest rose and fell with her efforts.

Next she felt his neck for a pulse. When she couldn't find one on the right, she checked the left. No pulse. Julie moved quickly down to the man's chest, pushing his open shirt aside and placing her hands over the lower half of his sternum.

She paused a split second when she saw the bruising under her hands. She didn't want to cause him any more damage. *Nonsense,* she thought instantly, pressing down firmly to send life-giving blood from his heart to his vital organs. *What were a few more bruises compared to death?*

"Hey!" Julie called out to some nurses who were pushing a stretcher toward the surgical suites. "I could use a hand!"

"I could use a dozen myself right now," one muttered in reply as he held pressure on a young boy's leg while a puddle of blood oozed out onto the sheet below. "Hang on, and we'll be right back."

With determination, Julie continued on. Of course, the boy needed immediate attention. His fresh, young life lay before him like a clean sheet of paper while this old man's life was nearly spent.

It wasn't her place, though, to say who would live and who would die. It was her place to try and save them all. If she had any say in the matter, this old man would live. If for no other reason, she decided, than for his young granddaughter. Memories of another eight-year-old girl and another freakish accident haunted her. Even now, she wondered if the medical personnel in attendance there had tried hard enough. Perhaps if they had tried one more push of medication. Perhaps if they had tried another minute or two of CPR. Perhaps . . . no! Julie shook her head.

That was the past, and there was no going back. Besides, getting all teary-eyed wasn't going to help her now. She had to keep her wits about her. In fact, it was time to stop and assess the patient again. She paused long enough to determine that his pulse and respirations had not returned spontaneously. She continued her efforts . . . fifteen compressions, two breaths, fifteen compressions, two breaths.

Moments later, Fern appeared with a portable crash cart. Julie sighed with relief, but the charge nurse passed right by. Julie stared after her. "Hey, Fern! Where are you going with that thing?"

"To the waiting room," Fern called over her shoulder. "We've got patients stacked up in there, and one of them just went down."

"I have a Code Blue of my own here. Any chance of getting help?"

"Hang in there, and I'll send someone."

Julie frowned as Fern and the precious crash cart disappeared around the corner. She wasn't going to give up. She wasn't. Fifteen compressions, two breaths, fifteen compressions, two breaths. She could go on forever if necessary.

As she worked, Julie thought it ironic that she was spending her final day at Mercy Hospital like this. It was a fitting tribute to endless hours spent doing much the same thing. Moments like this made her all the more ready to say goodbye to this place, to sever her final tie with the city, to embark upon this crazy scheme of hers.

But first, she had to struggle against all odds to keep this old man alive. A doctor appeared with a syringe in his hand, and Julie felt a surge of hope. "Doctor Giovanni, over here! I'm just about dying, and my patient isn't doing much better."

"Hang in there," he replied as he, too, dashed by. "A pregnant girl in the trauma room is delivering. I'll see what I can do in a minute."

"Thanks a lot," Julie murmured under her breath.

"In the meantime," the doctor shouted across the crowded hallway, "you'd better start praying."

All too accustomed to religious jokes since joining the Mormon church six months ago, Julie simply rolled her eyes. In fact, it was a cardiac arrest patient much like this one who had first introduced her to the Church. Help came quickly that time, though. Elder Montague had been transported to the critical care unit within a half hour of his collapse.

Julie could still remember the reaction of the missionary's wife all those months ago. Instead of losing control, she had simply gone to a corner of the room and prayed. Julie had been amazed by the feeling of strength that had entered her own being shortly thereafter.

After her shift, she had decided to check on them both, and had found Sister Montague in the waiting room. Her husband was doing fine, she said. She couldn't thank Julie enough for her efforts.

"It was my pleasure," Julie had insisted. "I should be thanking you for your prayers. I wish that I could gain such power from a prayer."

"You can," the woman replied with a knowing smile.

Those simple statements had led to several heart-to-heart talks between Julie and her newfound friends. Those, in turn, had led to three weeks of missionary discussions, which had led to a baptismal date. Julie embraced everything about the Church with open arms, especially the plan of salvation. After years of hopelessness, she couldn't explain the comfort it brought her.

If this old man dies, she thought as she shook memories of the past from her mind, he would see his granddaughter again someday. Did he know that? More importantly, did his granddaughter know that? Did they have the light of the gospel in their lives?

Julie couldn't speak for the old man, but she had the gospel in her life now, so she decided to take the doctor's advice. As she continued the regular compressions and intermittent respirations, she prayed—for strength, for endurance, and for help to arrive quickly.

"All right, Craig," Dr. Giovanni returned and scooted her aside, "let's see what you've got here."

Julie gave a brief report as she relinquished her spot at the man's chest to an orderly. Her arms were ready to collapse, and her lungs burned from the endless vigil. Still, she hoped her actions had not been in vain. The man just had to live . . . he just had to!

She held her breath as a therapist slipped a tube into the man's trachea, then crossed her fingers as a nurse slid a large needle into a vein and another hooked up a heart monitor. Julie silently prayed again as the doctor quickly scanned the EKG strip it spat out.

"V-fib, folks," he reported excitedly. "Keep it up."

Julie sighed with relief. Ventricular fibrillation, an ineffective rhythm of cardiac contraction, was better than no rhythm at all. Her efforts hadn't been in vain. She silently thanked the Lord, then asked for continued support from heaven for the man.

"I think this fellow has a chance," Giovanni continued, "if we can get his old ticker to cooperate. Draw up some lidocaine, and see how much power this old generator can muster up. Ready for cardioversion? All right, everyone, stand back. Clear!"

The lights dimmed down to almost nothing, but after the cardiac shock was delivered, the readout on the heart monitor made Julie smile. The man was going to be fine. His granddaughter's birthday party would perhaps need to be delayed for a few days, but it wouldn't be ruined.

Things were quieter throughout the emergency center now. Most of the patients had been admitted or discharged or taken to the morgue. Few still lingered in the emergency room, and the nurses were relaxing. Surviving a disaster like this was just another day's work.

Knowing there was nothing more to do there, Julie decided to return to the locker room. As she turned to leave, Julie heard her name. Dr. Giovanni stood in the hallway flashing a thumbs-up sign. "Good work, Craig. Heaven must have heard your prayers today 'cuz this old boy is going to be fine."

She smiled. "What did you expect? It's Easter, the perfect day for new life and miracles." And with that, the electricity flickered back on, washing the room in bright, glorious light.

Easter was being observed more traditionally in the farming community of Birch Creek, Idaho. One by one, vehicles made their way along the winding back roads with a single destination in mind: a small, country church upon a hillside. Churchgoers greeted each other warmly as they straggled inside.

One muddy Jeep snaked its way through the crowded parking lot without stopping. It slipped onto a quiet lane behind the church and disappeared. The occupant of that Jeep hadn't been to church in five years. And dressed in faded jeans and a weathered leather jacket, he apparently wasn't going to start today. Instead he made his way up to a small, fenced cemetery.

Pulling over to the side of the road, he paused for a while before turning off the engine. He sighed heavily as he reached over to the empty passenger seat and picked up a delicate white rosebud.

He stepped out of the Jeep and stood still for the longest time. The forgotten flower dangled precariously from his fingertips as he looked straight ahead, a battered cowboy hat tipped low over his eyes. He seemed totally oblivious to the striking scenery of the pristine valley that surrounded him.

He didn't notice the black and white dairy cows grazing on foothills behind him. He didn't smell the earthy, mountain loam, freshly plowed for spring planting. He didn't hear sacred hymns filtering up from the church below. He didn't see sunlight dancing off Birch Creek's namesake as it cascaded along its rocky path on its journey to meet the river.

What Pine Valley lacked in size, his father had always said, it made up for in beauty. Mark Jackson was usually the first to agree, but he didn't seem to notice or care on this particular morning. He travelled to the cemetery as a pilgrimage of sorts. For five years, he had marked each passing holiday, birthday, anniversary of that fateful day—the day his life turned upside-down–this way.

With slow, heavy steps, Mark crossed over to a small headstone in his family's plot. As he replaced a crumpled rosebud with the fresh one, he didn't think about the grave. He never did that. He didn't think about anything. And he felt nothing . . . nothing but numbness. Five years of numbness.

Mark's life resembled the crumpled flower in his hand—dried, shriveled, wasted. It was time to get going again, but he wasn't sure how to start. The numbness was protective . . . comfortable. If he didn't abandon the numbness, there would be no more pain. Deep inside, he knew there would be no happiness either, but he wasn't ready yet.

Stretching, Mark glanced around and noticed well, not exactly the beauty of the day, but rather the lack of rain. *Not a bad day to plant the corn,* he thought. *Keep working, keep busy.* He tossed the old rosebud aside and returned to the Jeep. Happiness would have to wait.

As Julie returned to the locker room, she remembered why she had chosen nursing as a career in the first place. It felt wonderful to make such an impact on a life. And there was an eight-year-old girl out there who wouldn't have to cry herself to sleep tonight. Yes, her efforts had been worthwhile!

If only cleaning out my locker could be so rewarding, Julie thought as she stubbed a high-heeled toe at the clutter that tumbled out. Crumbled candy wrappers, unused alcohol swabs, empty pop cans, and old magazines littered the floor. What a mess! Over the years, her locker had been an easy target for the often-rushed transition between nurse and civilian.

Before starting up again, Julie removed the lab coat and threw it into a hamper with a grimace. Oh, how she was tired of Mercy Hospital's green. She hoped her next place of employment would have different colored uniforms, or maybe even prints. Could she be so lucky?

Shrugging, Julie went to work. She was dusting off the empty shelves when the door to the locker room opened behind her. As the sweet scent of hyacinths reached her, Julie turned and literally flew into a pair of outstretched arms. She was enveloped into the ample bosom of her dearest friend and mentor, Vonda Nixon.

"Oh, Vonda!" Julie cried as she gazed up at the familiar face of a black woman in her late fifties. "What are you doing here?"

"I came to say goodbye, child," Vonda answered in the raspy baritone that was music to Julie's ears.

"You're supposed to be on vacation!" Julie protested. "Sipping exotic drinks and flirting with sailors in the middle of the Caribbean!"

"Oh, what's an old woman like me gonna do with sailors? I got tired of fighting off all those old fogies, so I cashed in the rest of my cruise for a ticket home."

Julie smiled at the image of her friend, far from a bikini knockout, fighting off "old fogies." She had several chins, her short, dark hair was peppered with gray, and her eyes were lined with wrinkles. Furthermore, her bikini would require more fabric than a tent. But Julie loved her dearly.

Vonda plopped down on a nearby bench. "I can't believe you're really going to go through with this move, child."

"Well, believe it," Julie replied as she scooted the trash can over beside Vonda, then swept up the last of the clutter on the floor with her hands. "I just have to finish here, then call a cab for the airport."

"Your aunt Stella isn't taking you in that fancy limo of hers?"

"No, she couldn't get away from the gallery," Julie sighed.

"I'll bet," Vonda replied drily. "She still opposes your decision?"

"Yeah, she thinks I've lost my mind."

"Well, I must admit that I have a few doubts about this wild scheme of yours myself, child." Vonda shifted on the narrow bench. "But you'll be fine. All your arrangements made?"

"My flight leaves at three," Julie stood and stretched her cramped legs. "And the Montagues will meet me when I land."

"And when do you head north from there?"

"In a week or two. They have made arrangements for a few sightseeing tours, I believe."

"You have a place to stay when you get there?" Vonda asked as she absentmindedly picked through the trash can.

"I can thank Ma Bell for both my job interview and my apartment. All the arrangements were made over the phone."

Vonda pulled a picture out of the garbage and wrinkled up her nose at it. "You aren't just running away, are you, child? Mr. LaRosa here isn't worth that much trouble."

"No," Julie returned quickly, glancing at the torn photograph. Her relationship with Vinny LaRosa had ended in a less than friendly way, but he was definitely not the reason that she was leaving New York!

Julie glanced at the clock on the wall. Over the years, it had been a source of irritation . . . keeping her on the move, never letting her relax. Now was no exception. She felt like she was ready to go, but all of a sudden, it felt so very final. She smiled at Vonda, but her voice cracked with sadness. "I'd better call that cab now if I'm ever going to make it to La Guardia on time."

"You have my phone number? I won't rest until you call, child."

"I have it written down, just in case I get amnesia or something," Julie replied with a grin.

Vonda reached up and clasped Julie's hands tight within her own. *So many contrasts,* she thought, *yet so alike.* She felt like she was losing her own child. "God bless you, child. Now tell me just one more thing before you go. Why Idaho, of all places?"

"I wish I knew, Vonda. I really wish I knew."

Chapter Two

Julie felt uncomfortable on the Greyhound as it rumbled through northern Utah. It wasn't the lumpy seat or the odor of exhaust fumes. It was her outfit. Amid muted hues of brown and gray, her kimono-style jacket of bright red and pink and yellow splashes stood out like a sore thumb.

Julie feigned sleep to ignore the leers of those around her, but her thoughts were far too active for the real thing. Her final destination, the small town of Oakwood in southern Idaho, was less than three hours away! She tingled with excitement or was it her nerves?

The last two weeks with her friends, the Montagues, had been hectic. From the moment her flight touched down in Salt Lake, they had whisked her off on a sightseeing extravaganza . . . from Temple Square to Saltair, from Moab to Wendover, from St. George to Park City. Mindful of Brother Montague's health, Julie tried to slow them down, but to no avail.

Of all the things Julie saw, she loved the wide open spaces the best. She couldn't get enough of the western desert, the mountains, or the stars! Even the city itself, as well as its suburbs, seemed open and friendly. She didn't miss New York at all.

Julie's rambling thoughts were interrupted by a repetitious clicking sound. What on earth? *Click, click, click.* Unable to come up with an explanation for the noise, Julie opened one eye just a crack.

She saw knitting needles. And their owner, an elderly woman, was seated next to her. Wispy, white curls encircled the woman's wrinkled face, and vein-covered hands deftly jabbed pink yarn into submission. Julie saw a lively spark in the clear, blue eyes that peered over a small pair of bifocals.

"Sorry to wake you, dear," the woman apologized as she pulled on the yarn to untangle it.

Julie wasn't used to people being so open. Cautiously, she answered, "Oh, don't worry. I wasn't asleep."

As the elderly woman's gaze fell upon Julie's attire, she said, "You know, I admire someone with the spunk to wear what they want."

Was that a compliment? Julie smiled weakly. Undaunted, the woman continued, "You meet the most interesting people on a bus, you know."

Julie nodded.

"My children hate my taking the bus. They say it isn't safe. But at my age and with these for weapons," she shook a knitting needle, "what's going to happen?"

Without a response from Julie, her neighbor continued. "My name is Emma Parsons, and I've been south for the winter. I'm headed back to the family home in Logan for the summer. St. George is simply too hot after mid-May, you know."

Julie finally found her voice. "It's nice to meet you, Mrs. Parsons. I'm Julie Craig."

"Oh, you're from New York! I can tell by your accent. I was raised in New Jersey. . . ."

With her words travelling as fast as her knitting needles, time passed quickly. Nothing escaped Mrs. Parsons' watchful eye or peppery tongue, and her astute observations kept Julie in stitches. Julie even found herself talking about her life in the city and her recent conversion to the Church. The persistent Mrs. Parsons, for all her prattle, possessed a listening ear.

As they passed through a canyon, Julie was enthralled by the beauty of the scenery: craggy peaks topped with snow; fresh, grassy meadows; the sparkling blue of a clear lake. Soon their ascent turned into a descent, and the deeply-wooded hillsides gave way to a large wide valley. Farmland, dotted with quaint homes and barns, dominated the scenery.

"Logan at last!" Mrs. Parsons exclaimed as the knitting needles came to a rest. "It feels good to be home again. Now Oakwood isn't much further. Another canyon, and you'll be in Pine Valley."

"I can't wait," Julie replied.

Mrs. Parsons tucked her knitting into her bag, then rose to her feet. "You must stop and visit when you come shopping in Logan. I'll be interested to hear if you've discovered why you felt so inspired to move out west."

Indeed, Julie thought as she promised to visit soon. Over the months, she too had often wondered why here, why now. She couldn't explain it, but she knew that this was something she had to do.

The bus pulled away, and she watched a waiting throng embrace Mrs. Parsons. *Family*, Julie thought. Oh, how she longed to belong to one. A real one, she added as she thought of her aunt.

As the bus pulled out onto the road again, Mrs. Parsons' seat was taken by a man who reminded Julie of New York the unwashed who haunted the halls of Mercy Hospital in hopes of a free meal. Julie adjusted her kimono as she concentrated on the passing scenery. More farmland, small towns, another canyon. The open spaces made Julie's head swim.

Alone with her thoughts, Julie felt a sudden surge of panic. What was she getting herself into here? A small town like Oakwood would be as foreign to her as the moon. Oh, she hoped her decision was based on inspiration, not indigestion or anything.

Even though it was Saturday, Mark wasn't getting much accomplished. He'd been stuck in the mud twice once in the Jeep and once on the tractor. Now the old farm relic had a flat tire. He removed it and pulled out a rusty nail with disgust. *Good grief, what else can go wrong?* he muttered to himself.

Mark threw the tire into the back of his Jeep, then headed to the barnyard to tell someone he was going to town to get it fixed. Jackson Acres, as they called their farm, was a family venture. With young ones to support, it was his brother Steve's main source of income. To Mark, it was more of a hobby. It was something to keep him busily distracted from the numbness of his life.

As he approached the haphazardly placed farm buildings, Steve and his three boys arrived from another field on four-wheeled ATVs. Sixteen-year-old Troy was old enough to drive one with Tommy, twelve, sprawled out across the back rack. Little Thad was sitting behind his dad, holding on for dear life. They were all sweaty and dirty from a morning of hard work.

"Time for lunch!" Steve called out as he stopped on a graveled area behind his house. "Want to join us?"

"Thanks anyway," Mark responded, stepping out of the Jeep. "The John Deere has a flat, and I'm headed into town to get it fixed."

"A flat, huh?" Steve pulled off his work gloves. "Get much plowed?"

"Not enough," Mark replied as little Thad flew off the four-wheeler, across the yard, and into his arms.

"Bring me a treat, plea'th, Uncle Mark!" he lisped with enthusiasm. "Th'omething chocolate. Plea'th!"

Mark agreed, then set him down and ruffled his hair before climbing back into the idling Jeep. All his nephews were special, Mark thought as he headed down the highway, but Thad was his favorite. As his mind wandered, he refused to allow the memory of yet another child to filter into his thoughts.

He took the tire to Fielding's Implement and was told that there was a waiting line. *Great,* he sighed. After getting candy bars for the boys, he decided to get some lunch. He went to the Polar Freeze on Main Street where a giggling teenager at the counter was concentrating more on talking on the telephone than on taking his order.

Finally, Mark got his food and slipped into a nearby booth. Pulling wrapped items from the sack, he scowled at a familiar smell. A seaburger? He hated fish. The girl had messed up his order. What a totally wasted day!

"Next stop is Oakwood, Idaho," the driver's voice crackled over the loudspeaker. "We'll arrive in five minutes."

At last, Julie sighed as she craned her head to see her new home from the window. Oakwood was nestled in the center of a cozy little basin called Pine Valley. As they entered the area, Julie had seen farmland stretched out like a patchwork quilt. Now farmhouses were giving way to quiet neighborhoods, then a small business district. It all looked so quaint . . . the bowling alley, the small motel, the hometown bakery. They passed a single movie theater, a grocery store, and a florist. Julie tried to drink in every detail.

The road paralleled railroad tracks on the left. Several tall, slender buildings sat near the tracks. They reminded Julie of miniature skyscrapers without windows. Although they were clearly marked "Pine Valley Grain Growers," Julie could only wonder what they were.

The people Julie saw on the sidewalks looked casual and friendly. They waved or spoke to each other as they passed. Most sported cowboy hats and boots. And everyone wore blue jeans—not a business suit or designer dress in sight. Amazing!

The bus turned left at the only traffic light in town, circled the block, and pulled back onto Main Street heading south. It stopped before a two-story building with a square marquee, proudly bearing the simple word "HOTEL" in large block letters. A Greyhound sign dangled from chains outside.

What luck, Julie thought. Her apartment wasn't ready yet, so she could stay here until it was. She left the bus, then helped the driver unload her things. She had accumulated quite a few bags, in addition to her carry-on, during her time with the Montagues.

As the bus lumbered off, leaving behind a puff of black

exhaust, Julie bent to pick up her things. The bus turned right at the corner, apparently to circle the block once again and continue its northward route. Julie didn't notice. She was having quite a time getting all her things in hand at once.

The bus was well out of sight before Julie stood and turned to enter the hotel. She paused with a frown. The doors were padlocked shut, and the windows were boarded up. The paint on the "HOTEL" sign was badly chipped, and the Greyhound sign was rusted. The place looked like it hadn't been open for years.

Now what? By habit, Julie ran a hand through her straight, shoulder-length hair and looked around. She was alone in a strange place, but it didn't look particularly threatening. Compared to New York, the town of Oakwood appeared downright tame.

Spotting a pay phone across the street outside a fast food place, Julie decided to call a cab to take her to the nearest motel. Out of habit, she looked both ways before stepping off the curb although the traffic seemed light. So with her suitcase and shopping bags in tow, Julie started to cross.

By the time he had finished the fish sandwich with its soggy fries, Mark was in a foul mood. Setting his half-finished Pepsi on the dashboard, he climbed into the Jeep and slammed the door. He sure hoped the tire was ready, because he really wanted to get something accomplished before nightfall.

Pulling out of the parking lot, he focused on the oncoming traffic to his left. As a spot opened, he gunned the gas pedal impatiently to enter the lane of traffic. Turning his head to the right, he saw a flash of bright flowers bolt in front of him . . . right in the middle of the street!

Swerving to miss the flowers, he had a head-on collision with a suitcase instead. He didn't actually hit its owner, but the jolt sent her sprawling and the contents of the suitcase flying. As he threw on his brakes, his Pepsi overturned, splashing down the front of him.

Mark cursed as he swung out of the Jeep and looked around. He cursed the Pepsi. He cursed the upended pedestrian, a brunette stranger he didn't recognize. He cursed the flat tire, the seaburger, and his whole wasted day. The girl just looked up at him from the pavement with a dazed expression.

She was dazed. One minute she was walking toward a telephone booth, and the next, she was on the ground with her clothes scattered all around her and some crusty, old farmer yelling obscenities at her. Who was this hayseed anyway?

From her precarious position, Julie looked up at him and saw a surprising thing. Blue eyes . . . beautiful blue eyes squinting at her from under the rim of an old cowboy hat. *It's too bad,* she thought slowly, *that they're wasted on an ornery old farmer.*

"Are you all right?" he barked down as her.

"What happened?" she managed in return, pushing hair from her face as she tried to stand. She didn't think she was hurt, but she teetered back and forth anyway until a pair of strong hands reached down, grasped her by the shoulders, and held her secure.

Despite his kind actions, Mark was fuming. "What were you doing in the middle of the street, lady? The traffic is awful this time of day."

Julie looked around doubtfully. "It didn't look too bad to me."

"Where are you from?" he asked caustically as he too surveyed the number of cars on the street. "Mars?"

"Actually, I'm from New York."

"Figures," he muttered and dropped his hands from her shoulders like hot potatoes. Julie had regained enough composure to remain upright. He laughed bitterly. "I'd think someone from a city would know how to cross a street properly."

"I know enough," she said pointedly as she adjusted her kimono, "to know that a pedestrian has the right-of-way—in most states, that is."

"Humph!"

Without further comment, he grabbed her suitcase and started stuffing her clothes into it with vigor. *A tourist,* he thought sourly as he avoided the more delicate items on the ground. That's all they needed. The city slicker had no doubt come to view country folks like exhibits at a zoo.

Julie was used to cool indifference in New York, but she rarely had been the object of outright anger. What had she done to this farmer anyway? He was the one who had hit her! None too gently, she retrieved her bag from him and gathered her remaining belongings from off the asphalt.

"You hurt?" He didn't appear particularly concerned.

"Not that I know of," was her curt reply.

"Need an ambulance?"

"If you could just call me a cab, I'll gladly get out of your hair."

Mark snorted. A cab. The city girl wants a cab. In his best backwoods accent, he informed her, "Ain't no cabs in Oakwood, ma'am. Just us country bumpkins here with a few horseless carriages."

With all her bags in tow, she huffed, "Well, point me in the direction of the nearest motel—I suppose you have one of those—and I'll walk."

Mark felt the tiniest twinge of responsibility for her predicament. A crowd of spectators was forming, and he scowled with disgust. The sooner they got out of there, the better. Unexpectedly, he picked up Julie, bags and all, and headed toward the Jeep.

Caught off guard, Julie found herself unceremoniously dumped into the passenger seat of a Jeep. In a flash, Mark was in the driver's seat, quickly pulling away from the scene. *This old farmer isn't as frail as he looks*, she thought. *In fact, he seems pretty strong.*

"Just one motel in Oakwood," he grumbled as they headed south. "Better take you there and make sure you arrive in one piece."

Retracing her recent route on Main Street, Julie paid little attention to her surroundings this time. Instead she glanced sideways at her unlikely knight in shining armor. He was as crusty as they came.

His face was deeply tanned, and his hair was sticking out at odd angles from under his cowboy hat. His clothes were worn, and his boots were caked with mud. His blue eyes were squinting in a fierce scowl. *All he needs to complete the picture*, she decided with an inward smile, *is a piece of straw to chew on.*

"Thank you for the ride to the motel," she said brightly.

"Yeah, sure," he mumbled, then a strained silence returned.

"Oakwood looks like quite a nice town."

"Humph!"

Cantankerous old coot, Julie thought and gave up trying to be polite. She was tired and hungry. She wanted a long, hot bath. And she needed to call Vonda. What she didn't need was the cold shoulder treatment from a hayseed, but she was getting it, all right.

They reached the motel, and both were glad to part ways. *That girl and her big city ways*, thought Mark as he pulled away. She did things to his blood pressure! He wouldn't give her a second thought. Not at all. But he was halfway back to the farm before he remembered the tire.

Chapter Three

By Wednesday morning, Julie felt at home in her new apartment. Dressed in a navy blue suit with crisp white trim, she stood at the sink in the bathroom and styled her hair. She had an appointment to meet Mrs. Ward at the hospital at ten, and she didn't want to be late.

But as she looked in the mirror, she paused to ask herself the burning question again . . . *Why Oakwood?* So far, nothing had presented itself as a vital reason for her presence there, but she could wait. The most pressing issue at hand was getting settled into her new life.

After two nights at the motel, her apartment was ready on Monday morning. Julie's first thought upon seeing the Casa Grande apartments was that they didn't quite live up to their name. The entire complex consisted of two small buildings with four apartments each facing each other across a grassy play area. Parking stalls with storage sheds ran behind each building.

As she met her new landlady, Mrs. Ellsberg, Julie thought the woman looked vaguely familiar. She had round eyes that blinked rapidly, a pointed nose, and almost no chin. Her graying hair was pulled up sharply into a tight bun, and her figure was lumpy beneath a brown polyester dress that was two sizes too small.

Her voice had a scratchy, nasal quality as she read the contract, line by line, to Julie and gave her an hour's lecture on proper tenant behavior. Julie endured it with a patient smile. As the woman led Julie to her new apartment, her strut created a visual image that startled Julie.

That was it! Julie had seen that strut before . . . at a petting zoo! As she said her prayers that night in her new home, Julie asked for forgiveness—for not going to church on the previous day, for being too tired to read her scriptures, and for thinking that Mrs. Ellsberg looked like a chicken.

Julie had shipped most of her things ahead, so she spent the next two days unpacking. As she left now for her appointment, she paused a moment at the door and smiled. *Not too bad.*

The place came furnished, but a few personal touches—plants from the florist, pieces of her own pottery, poster prints from her aunt's art gallery—made all the difference. She had her potter's wheel in the spare bedroom and a faded photograph of her parents beside her bed. Inch by inch, it was beginning to feel like home.

I've even made a friend already, Julie thought as she walked through the play area and saw two blonde children playing in the sandbox as a young mother watched from a nearby bench. Spotting Julie, the woman called out, "Good luck today!"

"Thanks, Debbie."

Unlike that crusty, old farmer or even Mrs. Ellsberg, Julie had finally met someone in Oakwood that she didn't seem to bother, irritate, or annoy. They met the day Julie moved in, and the rapport between the two was instantaneous and natural.

"Hold your nose," the woman, a petite thing with long, black hair, had warned as she held a diaper pail at arm's length near the trash dumpster.

"Smells like a 'Code Brown,'" Julie joked.

"What? Oh, yeah. Hey, you must be the new girl from apartment #8."

"That's me. Julie Craig."

"I'm Debbie Ventura," she smiled eagerly. "I've never met anyone from New York before."

"How did you know . . . ?"

"Oh, it's a small town. Not much happens. Everyone knows everything about everyone."

And it wasn't long before Julie knew most of Debbie's life history. She wasn't from Oakwood, but her husband was, so they had moved here not long after their wedding. Her husband, a truck driver, wasn't home much, leaving her to handle their two small children alone. She spent many of her weekends visiting family in Malad.

Julie waved goodbye, then walked to the hospital, arriving with a few minutes to spare. The one-story building sat directly in the center of a block next to medical offices and a drug store. Julie also noticed a funeral parlor nearby. She hoped it was only a coincidence.

Once inside, Julie found herself in a small lobby with two long halls stretching out on either side like a "V". A white-haired volunteer in a pink jacket sat behind a small reception desk. She greeted Julie cheerily. "Good morning! May I help you?"

Julie looked around uncertainly. "I'm to meet Mrs. Ward here at ten."

"I'll find her for you. Wait here."

Julie paced until the head nurse arrived. Julie took one look and decided Mrs. Ward was a picture of the perfect nurse. Her spotless white uniform was adorned by a black name tag and several small pins. Her short hair was topped by a boxy, white cap, and reading glasses hung from her neck. The polish on her shoes would have made the nuns at Mercy proud.

She ushered Julie into her office, which was equally neat and clean. Flipping through a file bearing Julie's name, she spoke clearly, "Julie Craig, we meet at last."

"It's my pleasure, Mrs. Ward."

"Kathleen, please. We're fairly casual here."

After a little small talk, Kathleen got down to business. Julie soon had all the necessary paperwork completed. They discussed her orienting schedule, pay scale, and benefits.

Everything was as Julie expected until her new employer cleared her throat nervously and said, "I have a favor to ask, Julie. I know we offered you a full-time day shift, and I'm not backing out. But one of the night shift nurses just underwent surgery. It would help a lot if you could fill in for her, just for a couple of weeks."

"Well," Julie tried not to sound disappointed, "I was hoping to lead some sort of a normal life."

"I know what you mean," Kathleen replied. "Night shifts make you feel like a mole, don't they? Well, it's up to you. If you'd rather not. . . ."

Julie felt trapped. She was indebted to her new employer, who had hired her sight unseen over the phone. Julie wanted to prove that she could be a team player, so she agreed to the temporary position.

"Good," Kathleen sighed. "You're a lifesaver. Now for a tour of the facilities."

The hospital was clean and well-equipped, though small. Julie decided the entire thing would fit inside the emergency center at Mercy with room to spare. But she liked it all the same. It was, in a word, quaint.

Extended care facilities filled the long hall to the left, along with administrative offices, a dining area, and the physical therapy section. An acute care area occupied the hallway to the right with one nurse's station serving its twenty beds. There was one operating suite and one delivery room. The lab was housed in a single room, as were the pharmacy and X-ray departments.

The emergency room, where Julie would be stationed, was located at the end of that hall. Three stretchers in the single room were separated by striped curtains. Modern monitoring and resuscitating equipment sat next to several medical antiques Julie had never seen before.

A blonde nurse manned the desk, greeting Julie with a smile. A radio behind her crackled coded messages between the town's patrolling police officers. As she was introduced, Julie was glad to see the nurse wore a printed scrub uniform. No more greens!

They returned to Kathleen's office, where the head nurse confirmed the final details of Julie's position. They shook hands in parting, then Julie thought to ask, "Oh, but what about the uniforms?"

"I almost forgot. Even though I like white, you're allowed to wear colors or prints as long as they're clean and pressed. White athletic shoes are also acceptable."

"That sounds good, but, I mean . . . where are they?"

"Where?" Kathleen seemed puzzled. "You don't have your own?"

"At Mercy, uniforms were provided."

"An allowance?"

"No, the actual uniforms," Julie explained. "They belonged to the hospital. We changed into them for our shift and threw them into a hamper as we left. You don't do that here, I assume."

"No. Actually, we're responsible for our own uniforms. They're tax-deductible, you know. You don't have any of your own?"

"None."

"Well, let's see," Kathleen thought for a moment, then snapped her fingers. "I'll get you a couple from the operating room. Take them home until you get some of your own."

"I'd appreciate that. Where can I get some around here?"

"Oh, Logan or Pocatello would be the closest places. I usually go down to Logan for mine."

"I see," Julie nodded as Kathleen scurried off in the direction of the operating room.

She returned with a stack of green scrubs, and Julie left the hospital with mixed feelings. She tried to be thankful for this solution to her unexpected predicament. But green uniforms? Yikes! She would have to get some of her own, and fast.

Debbie and her children were still in the play area when Julie returned. Plopping down on the bench beside her friend, Julie kicked off her shoes. "Those heels weren't made for walking."

"How did it go?" her new friend asked.

"Pretty good, but tell me, how does one get to Logan from here?"

"On the road," Debbie teased.

"Funny," Julie moaned, then punched at the uniforms on her lap. "I need to go shopping real soon. I suppose I could take the bus."

Debbie chuckled. "How many days do you plan on spending there?"

"Just a couple of hours. Why?"

"Well, the bus only goes south on Tuesdays, and north on Saturdays."

"I guess that wouldn't work," Julie admitted forlornly.

"Most people drive down. Don't you have a car?"

When Julie shook her head, her friend offered, "I'd let you borrow mine, but it's been making a funny noise. Chip said not to drive it until he can take a look."

"That's okay. I don't drive anyway."

"Don't as in can't?" Debbie sounded astonished. "How do you get anywhere?"

"In Oakwood, I've been walking."

"Yeah, nothing is very far away in this town, is it?" Debbie giggled. "But in New York? You never drove a car?"

"Nope," Julie answered, pushing hair away from her face with a habitual flip. "I either took a subway, a train, a taxi, a bus, or my aunt's limo. It's too expensive to keep a car in New York City, so I never learned to drive."

"Rough life," Debbie replied with mock sarcasm. "I can't believe that you don't drive. Personally, I've been driving since I was fourteen. Listen, if you can wait that long, I've got an appointment in Logan in about two weeks. You can go down with me."

"Great," Julie replied sincerely. She could wear green uniforms for two more weeks if she knew the end of them was in sight.

They were interrupted by Debbie's children. Three-year-old Cody came on a dead run, his head covered with sand as he cried, "Mama! Bratty dump'd sand on me head."

Little Brandy squealed with delight, clapping her chubby

hands at the commotion she created. Julie couldn't help smiling. "Your kids are so cute, Debbie."

"Give Bratty 'pankin', Mama! Give her one now!"

"Yeah, real cute," Debbie moaned as she set out to restore peace to her small family. Julie was green with envy. *Someday*, she thought, *someday*.

Later that week, Mark's best friend, Rick Lee, called with good news. Mark drove up to Rick's ranch, on the edge of Birch Creek where the highway began its winding journey through Snow Canyon, to see for himself. Leaning over a fence at the ranch, Mark gave a low whistle of approval.

"Isn't she a beauty?" Rick elbowed Mark in the ribs as the tiny foal wobbled to its feet at the nudging of its mother, a chestnut mare.

Mark readily agreed, then looked around him and sighed. Rick's kids were playing noisily on a tree swing in the backyard. Rick's wife, Annie, was gathering wash off the clothesline as the aroma of Rick's dinner drifted towards them. This was the life.

This was where Mark's life would have been if fate had not decided otherwise. This is where he wanted to be—with a wife to love, kids to keep things lively, horses to tend instead of dairy cows. Mark took off his hat, wiped his brow with the back of his hand, and nodded toward the newborn. "You did a good job, Rick."

"Yup. She'll be a prize winner. Bring a pretty good price, too, if I decide to sell her." Rick beamed like a proud father. "Hey, when am I ever going to talk you into buying one of these animals?"

Mark would have loved to have a horse at Jackson Acres, but he didn't press the issue. His brother was in charge and had enough mouths to feed. *If I had my own place . . .* , Mark thought with a sigh. Humorously he retorted, "Spend my hard-earned money when I can come up here and ride for free? You should be paying me for exercising them!"

"Yeah? There are two chances of that, buddy."

"I know, slim and none." The sun was beginning its evening retreat, and Mark stretched away from the fence. "Evening chores aren't going to wait while I stand around here gossiping with the likes of you."

"Who you calling a gossip?" Rick grabbed for Mark's hat, but Mark was too quick. They wrestled and punched a little, just like when they were boys. Mark drove away feeling good.

The good feeling persisted until he paused by his grandparents' old farm, just north of the Birch Creek church. The land looked pretty good, but the house and the barnyard were neglected. His grandma would roll in her grave if she saw those weeds. And if his grandpa saw that peeling paint on the barn. . . .

Before Mark could drive away, Gus Gledhill, who leased the farm from Mark's mother, sauntered out the back door and spotted him. Now he'd really be late getting back, Mark groaned to himself as the tall, lean man ambled over. Gus had never, ever hurried in his life.

"How do?" Gus drawled slowly.

"Fine, and you?"

"Fair . . . pretty fair." Gus scratched his whiskered chin and added, "Been meaning . . . to call your ma. I have my eye . . . on buying . . . a piece of land . . . up north."

"Sounds good," Mark replied. Gus was always looking to buy his own land, but had never quite gotten around to it.

After several more minutes of slow-paced talk, Mark extracted himself from the conversation. He was surprised that Gus ever got a thing done at his leisurely pace. Waving goodbye, he sped down the road.

In his melancholy mood, though, Mark even envied Gus tonight. Martha Gledhill had a reputation for being one of the best cooks in town. All that waited for Mark tonight was a frozen T.V. dinner.

Julie paused and readjusted the two heavy grocery sacks she

was carrying. Her lack of transportation was getting old. She was tired of walking and more tired of carrying bags to and from the shops of Oakwood. And working night shifts all week made her just plain tired.

As she trudged along, she passed a sporting goods store. A red ten-speed bicycle in the window caught her eye. *Wheels!* Julie set the bags down and peered inside. The bike was used, but looked like it was good condition. The price was right. Could she?

She hadn't ridden a bike for years—since she was just a kid in the suburbs, but it wouldn't take long to remember again, would it? Anything would be better than walking. Julie ached to see the countryside. She couldn't get enough of the scenery or the wide open spaces. She wanted to get acquainted with everything about her new home!

On a whim, Julie went inside and bought the bike. The store owner, a bear of a man with a sandy beard, attached a wire basket onto the back for her. Now she could carry her shopping bags with ease.

Look out, Pine Valley! Julie was ready to explore!

Chapter Four

Julie spent an hour or two on the bike each day, suffering sore muscles only the first day or two. Armed with maps from the courthouse, she went south, east, north, and west, travelling dirt roads, paved roads, gravel roads, and sometimes no roads at all.

Farmland prevailed outside city limits, but she found streams and ponds, remnants of log cabins, and plenty of pine trees. The fresh breeze, the absolute quiet, the open spaces. . . . It was wonderful! One old man summed up her feelings by noting, "Ain't actually the end of the earth, but you can see it from here."

Unlike Vonda, Aunt Stella didn't laugh when Julie told her that. Certain that Julie was stranded in a wilderness, she sent weekly care packages from the finest shops in the city. The latest was a spandex biking outfit of neon green from Bloomingdale's.

Julie donned it one Saturday morning, then after surveying her appearance in the mirror, pulled an oversized T-shirt over it. *Much better for this conservative community,* she decided. She packed a lunch sack, filled her water bottle, then grabbed her maps off the table.

It had rained the previous night, and the morning air was fresh and cool as she swung the bike out of her parking stall. She rode north to the edge of town where the highway forked. A sign showed Preston and Pocatello to the west, Montpelier and Bear Lake to the east.

Julie had tried the western route, finding a ghost town. Consulting a map, she followed the road eastward with a fingertip. This time, she found a stretch called Antelope Flats. Crossing the Bear River on the map, she saw a place called Birch Creek, then another called Snow Canyon. Interested, Julie decided to try it.

She sailed through the flat area, looking for antelope in the sagebrush as she went. She didn't know what an antelope looked like, but she was sure it was some kind of animal. Well, fairly sure.

Soon Julie reached the river. The view from the bridge was breathtaking. A tangle of wild brush lined the river downstream. Upstream, water tumbled over rocks as the banks of the river steepened into rugged cliffs. A huge bird gliding overhead caught her eye.

Veering left, it circled lower and lower. Trying to keep it within view, Julie took off on her bike. Before long, she left the main highway and rode down a graveled road heading west where she could see it landing gracefully upon a telephone pole.

Julie stared. It had a white head and brown body. A bald eagle? The telephone pole was only a hundred yards from the road. She dropped her bike and slowly walked towards it, mesmerized by the sight, tingling with excitement. A bald eagle! The quiet morning air held a spell of magic.

"What the heck are you doing in the middle of my field?" A harsh voice broke the spell and nearly scared Julie to death.

A hand flew to her pounding heart as she turned to see the old farmer walking down the road towards her. It was so quiet, she hadn't realized anyone else was around. The eagle, undisturbed by the outburst, continued to look for its lunch.

As the man neared, Julie realized he was the same crusty, old farmer she had met on Main Street. Not him again! Not yelling at her . . . again! She couldn't have been less pleased to see anyone on the planet, perhaps with the exception of Vinny LaRosa.

Mark was equally displeased to see her. Who could be so idiotic as to trample through his field? There was actually very little damage done, but in his present mood, it took very little to irritate him.

He'd spent the morning stringing barbed wire. Of all the duties on the farm, fencing was his least favorite. But next week, cattle would come up this road for summer grazing in Butterfield Basin. Mark's intention was to keep the four-legged intruders off his crops.

He wasn't quick enough, though, to stop a two-legged intruder, he thought as he eyed the girl. Suddenly, he recognized her. *The girl from New York!* Mark was surprised that she was still around, but he wasn't at all surprised she was in the middle of his field. . . . *Trust a city girl for that.*

"What's the big idea, traipsing all over my crops?" he barked.

Julie looked down and, for the first time, realized where she was. Shifting her feet, she saw the remains of several small, green plants underfoot with more crumpled behind her. How did that happen?

"Oh no!" She leaned over and tried to restore the limp sprouts back into their original position. She failed.

"Forget it, lady. They're goners."

"I'm so sorry," she gushed. "I didn't realize that this was a field."

"Haven't you ever heard of trespassing, lady?"

Julie thought of the boarded-up windows and chained doors of condemned buildings. She had seen plenty of "No Trespassing" signs, but in the middle of nature? "I didn't see a sign," she hedged.

"That's because the fence is down," he grumbled, "but anyone with half a mind would know better."

Anyone with half a mind, Julie thought crossly as she tried to lift a muddy foot. She had every intention of getting out of there and fast, but with each labored step came an awful sucking sound as dark earth, still wet from the rain, clung to her shoes in large clumps. She was stuck!

"Stay there! I'll come get you," Mark commanded as his long strides brought him to her side. He resisted an urge to pick her up and throw her over his shoulder. After their last meeting, she'd really think he was a country bumpkin.

Instead, he held her firmly by the elbow and guided her back to the road. As they went, Mark realized he hadn't held a woman's arm in a long time. It felt soft and warm. Too soon almost, they reached dry ground.

"Thank you," Julie said sincerely, her temper softened. She began to scrape mud from her shoes, but only managed to collect more in her efforts.

"Here, let me," Mark finally offered. He squatted down and gently removed Julie's shoes. She stood in her stockings as he worked on the mess with his pocket knife.

As he did, she studied him. In a white T-shirt and St. Louis Cardinals baseball cap, he didn't look nearly as old, nor as crusty as she had thought. He wasn't as skinny either . . . lean, but strong, too. Only his eyes were as she remembered—a striking shade of blue.

"I'm surprised you're still around," Mark snorted as he glanced up briefly. "I thought you'd be back in the city by now. Haven't had enough of this small town?"

"Actually, no."

"You're not bored silly without all the lights and glamour?"

"Hardly," she looked around. "There are so many things here you'd never find in a city."

"Yeah?" he asked sarcastically. "Like what, lady?"

"That, for instance," Julie pointed to the bird. "Is it a bald eagle?"

Mark nodded. "Yeah, it is. You don't see those every day, even out here."

They both watched as the eagle rose in flight. With strong strokes, it headed towards the river. It dove, then rose with a silver trout writhing in its strong talons.

"Beautiful," Julie whispered in awe.

Mark turned to look at her as he nodded, then he quickly looked back toward the bird and nodded again. Her shoes were clean, and he helped her slip them on, tying them as if she were a child. He stood and put his work gloves back on.

"Thank you," Julie smiled. Vinny would have never cleaned her shoes. Actually, Vinny would have never walked into the muddy field to help her in the first place. Looking guiltily at Mark's not-too-clean boots, she apologized. "I'm sorry."

"Don't worry about these dirty old things, lady."

"I'm sorry about your potatoes, too."

"My what?"

Julie pointed at the flattened plants. "Your potatoes."

It took Mark a moment to understand. *Oh, yeah, Idaho . . . potatoes.* Again he groaned to himself. "It's corn, lady."

Julie looked doubtful. Didn't they grow corn in Iowa? There was so much she didn't understand. She shook her head and spotted some animals grazing on a nearby hill. "Hey, are those antelope?"

Mark swung around with interest, then laughed aloud. "Those are sheep, lady. You know, baa, baa."

"I thought sheep were woolly."

"They've been shaved for the summer, lady."

"Oh." Julie felt silly. Even so, how could she learn if she didn't ask? Pointing to a shimmer of water in the distance to the north, she said, "Is that Birch Creek?"

"Yeah," Mark nodded, "but it's pronounced 'crik,' not 'creek,' lady. That word grates on nerves like fingernails on a blackboard."

"I'll make you a deal," Julie replied with a look of determination. "I'll say 'crik' if you'll quit calling me lady. My name is Julie."

Mark had to admire her spunk. "Deal."

"And what can I call you?" she asked, then added to herself, *besides "that old coot."*

Mark grinned knowingly. "The name's Mark."

"Well, thanks for your help, Mark." Julie climbed back onto her bike. "And I really am sorry about the corn."

"Don't worry about it, la—uh, Julie."

Mark watched her ride back to the highway. She looked ridiculous on that bike . . . ridiculously cute. But how long would it take for her to tire of this sightseeing and return to the city? He removed his hat, wiped his brow, then went back to work.

The following Wednesday, Debbie and Julie drove to Logan for the scheduled appointment. Julie nibbled on one of Debbie's delicious chocolate chip cookies as they went. With her last bite, she said, "That cookie was heavenly."

"Have another," Debbie invitingly lifted up a plastic bag full of them. "I made plenty."

"I wish I could bake like that," Julie sighed wistfully.

"I'll give you the recipe."

"Thanks, but I haven't a molecule of cooking ability in my whole body," Julie admitted. "Hey, I met a guy named Mark a few days ago."

"A guy? Do I detect a spark of interest?"

"Oh, no, nothing like that. He's too old and ornery, but I wonder about him all the same. Do you know him?"

"I don't know too many of the locals yet myself," Debbie shrugged, "but we can ask Chip about him when we get back."

"All right."

Debbie's husband had returned to Oakwood in time to fix the car and tend the kids for Debbie's trip. Julie watched the two of them with a touch of envy. *How would it feel to be in love again?*

Once they reached Logan, Julie and Debbie had a fun, if busy, day. At the mall, they bought summer clothes for the kids, socks for Chip, and uniforms for Julie. Delighted to find so many different colors, Julie bought one in every shade, except green.

They had lunch at the Bluebird Cafe. On their way out, Debbie introduced Julie to a sinful treat: O'Aggie chocolate bars. *How on earth,* Julie wondered, *does Debbie stay so petite?*

During Debbie's appointment, Julie planned to visit with Mrs. Parsons. On the way to her house, they passed the temple. It was beautiful, Julie thought, its white, domed spires atop a building of purplish stone. This is the temple she would attend someday to be sealed to her family, she decided.

Mrs. Parsons' house, built around the turn of the century, had green carpet on the porch and geraniums in flower boxes at the windows. Julie rang the doorbell and was greeted almost immediately by a spirited embrace. With a flurry of chatter, Mrs. Parsons whisked her inside.

"Julie, it's so good to see you again. I thought you'd never come. How was the ride? I've been rushing around here all morning, getting things ready. Now come in and sit right down. We have so much to talk about."

Though Julie had never known her own grandparents, this felt like a grandma's house to her. The furnishings were dated, and an aroma of baking filled the air. A large Siamese cat sat on a cushion at the bottom of a long staircase with a polished bannister.

Julie didn't manage to get in a single word until she was seated in a parlor. The room was filled with knitting paraphernalia, various figurines of cats, and a ton of photographs. They covered the mantel, the piano, and most of the walls.

"That's Ming Ming," Mrs. Parsons introduced the cat, who was now rubbing itself on Julie's ankles. "I thought we would have tea. Well, not really tea, but you know what I mean."

She poured lemonade into tall glasses, then spread butter and fresh strawberry jam on thick chunks of bread. It tasted wonderful. To answer Julie's compliment, the older woman confessed to using frozen bread dough.

"Don't tell my kids, though. They would be shocked. Now tell me all about Oakwood."

The afternoon flew by. Julie felt more like a long lost granddaughter than a casual acquaintance from a bus trip. And at some point, Mrs. Parsons picked up her knitting.

"My granddaughter, Robyn, is due around Labor Day. I'm making a sweater for the babe. Let's see," she pointed to a photograph on the piano, "that one is Robyn. She lives in Wyoming, you know."

Before long, Julie had seen and heard about each picture in the room. Some were new, others were old and faded. There was Mrs. Parsons as a bride. There were pictures of her four children in various stages of development. There were a myriad of grandchildren, and even great-grandchildren. *Wouldn't it be great to belong to such a large family?* she sighed.

Julie's gaze stopped on a young man in cap and gown. Mrs. Parsons said the picture was taken of her grandson as he graduated from high school. His sandy blonde hair hung long on his neck, his smile was slightly crooked, and his blue eyes twinkled with mischief.

Not far away was another picture of the same young man. He was dressed in a white tuxedo and standing by a girl in a wedding gown. They were so young, Mrs. Parsons shook her head sadly. Julie agreed.

As they reached the last picture in the room, Debbie knocked on the door. Introductions were followed by small talk. Before they left, Mrs. Parsons invited Julie to her birthday party in June.

"At my age, I'm not sure how many more parties I'll be hosting, you know, so you won't want to miss it."

Julie agreed to attend. It was late afternoon as she and Debbie drove back into Pine Valley. Julie watched carefully as Debbie maneuvered the car along the winding road. All week, Julie had thought about getting her own car and the freedom to explore it would give her.

"Is that hard?" she asked as Debbie shifted gears.

"Not really."

"It looks complicated."

"Maybe at first, but soon it comes naturally."

"Where did you learn to drive?" Julie wondered. "I looked for driving schools in the yellow pages, but all I found were drive lines and drive-ins."

"Not surprising," Debbie laughed. "I took a driver's ed course in high school."

"High school, huh? Could I take lessons there?"

"All you can do is ask," Debbie said, then added, "I'd offer to teach you myself, but with Cody and Brandy in the car, we'd both be nervous wrecks."

Thanks to another nurse's bout of flu, Julie's first time alone in the emergency room turned out to be an evening shift instead of a midnight one. It was slow for a Friday, but then she was judging from New York standards. No stabbings, no gunshot wounds, no drug overdoses.

So far, she had seen three patients: an allergy shot, an insulin reaction, and a slight concussion. She would save more lives in New York, but there was a reason she was here. Maybe there was a life here that needed to be saved, and only she could do it. Sooner or later, she'd figure it out.

A doctor slipped through the automatic doors and joked, "Another busy day at the office?"

"Things are hopping, Dr. Bolinsky."

"Well, I'm needed in delivery. I was having one of the worst golf games in my career. Saved by the beeper."

Julie laughed as Dr. Bolinsky walked on through. Of the four doctors at the hospital, he was her favorite. After all, he had trained in New York. They remembered the same haunts. Like Julie, he had joined the Church, then moved his family closer to Zion.

Julie always thought a doctor could be judged by his handwriting. Dr. Poplin's was big and swirly, matching his ego. Dr. Mundy's looked like a seismograph gone awry. And Dr. Smythe couldn't even read his own handwriting. Dr. Bolinsky's, on the other hand, was neat and legible.

The automatic doors opened again, and a heavyset man with gray hair entered. He held one hand wrapped in a bloody dishtowel. Julie sprang to her feet and helped him onto a stretcher.

"What have we got here?" she asked, unwrapping the hand to expose a laceration across the palm.

"Just a scratch," he smiled sheepishly. "It wouldn't quit bleeding, so I thought I'd better come in."

Julie smiled reassuringly, probed at the wound, then applied a pressure dressing. "It doesn't look like you'll bleed to death, so let me get some information. Name?"

"Clyde Owens."

"Address?"

"243 North Main."

"Any significant medical history or allergies?"

"Healthy as a horse."

"Good thing you're not a horse, Mr. Owens," she teased, "or we'd have to shoot you, with a wound like that. Dr. Bolinsky's in delivery. He can take a look when he's done."

While they waited, Julie prepared a tray with syringes, a local anesthetic, suturing equipment, and clean gauze. The doctor came, sutured up the wound, then wrote some orders before he left. Not exactly a life in the balance, Julie thought as she cleaned up after him, but it felt good.

Julie gave Mr. Owens a supply of dressings to take home, then checked the orders. Drawing up a dose of tetanus vaccine, she announced with a grin, "Looks like I get to shoot you after all."

Mr. Owens just groaned in response.

Chapter Five

Oakwood High School dismissed at three-thirty, and Julie arrived shortly thereafter on Monday afternoon. As students straggled out, a driver's education car pulled away from the curb. Even though thoughts of taking driving lessons made her both excited and nervous, Julie hoped to be joining them soon.

As she entered the building, memories of her own school days flooded back. Her eyes travelled past the long rows of lockers to the large trophy case. Taped across its glass was a brightly painted sign announcing the upcoming senior class trip.

The principal's office sat to the left of the foyer. The desks in the outer office were cluttered, but vacant. Soft whistling came from the slightly opened door to the inner office. Should she disturb the principal? What if he was a grouch? Most of the people in Oakwood were friendly, but there were a few . . . like an ornery, old farmer named Mark.

Julie took a deep breath and knocked. She was answered by a voice bellowing, "Come in!" She peered inside timidly, then sighed with relief when she saw who sat behind the massive desk.

It was Mr. Owens, using his bandaged hand as a paperweight while he scribbled awkwardly with the other. He set the papers aside before looking up. He recognized Julie immediately.

"What a surprise!" he sprang to his feet and offered her a chair. "It's nice to see you again."

"How is your hand?"

"A little sore. You're making a house call?"

"Not exactly," Julie shifted uncomfortably in her seat. "I was wondering if you might help me with something."

"What's on your mind?"

"Well, I need driving lessons. I've talked to a number of people in town, and they all say that they learned in high school."

Mr. Owens looked baffled. "You don't drive?"

"No, and I know I'm a bit older than your other students, but I'm willing to do whatever it takes."

"Hmm," Mr. Owens frowned. "Our courses are funded by taxpayers' money. There are stiff regulations on who can enroll."

"I'm sorry to bother you," Julie rose to leave.

"Hold on," he motioned for her to sit back down. "Perhaps we can work something out. I have three certified teachers here. Maybe private lessons could be arranged."

"That would be great."

"Well, let's see." Mr. Owens rocked back and forth in his swivel chair while he thought. "Mr. Brenchley is our track coach, and Mr. Ross' wife just had a new baby. That leaves Mr. Jackson."

"Mr. Jackson?"

"He doesn't teach in the summer—too busy on the farm, you know. Maybe he could teach you in the next few weeks before school gets out. Only one way to find out."

Mr. Owens left the office and returned moments later. He was followed by a young teacher in a tweed jacket and dark slacks. He was loosening his tie and focusing on what the principal was saying as they approached. Julie got a good look at him.

He looked nice enough. He was tall, lanky, and clean shaven. His dark blonde hair was thick and wavy. As the men entered the room, they were laughing. Julie thought his smile was warm and inviting.

The thought of spending time with a good-looking man like this wasn't unpleasant. She wasn't in the market for romance, but a little flirtation couldn't hurt. After all, she'd grown quite rusty in that area since her breakup with Vinny.

As Mr. Owens introduced Julie Craig to Mark Jackson, he was

unaware of the undercurrent of electricity that ran between them. He didn't see Julie's shocked look as she recognized those blue eyes. Nor did he notice those eyes narrow as they identified the girl Mark had been trying to forget all week.

"When I told Mr. Jackson about a beautiful, young girl in my office who needed lessons," he chuckled, "he was more than willing to help out."

That was before I knew it was the city girl who needed lessons, Mark thought crossly. *I can't believe that a sophisticated city girl can't drive.*

Help me out? Julie wondered. *He'd just love to help me out of a speeding train. Or a speeding driver's ed car.*

"You *live* here?" Mark snarled.

"Sure do!" Julie replied brightly.

As Mr. Owens fumbled for something in a desk drawer, he asked, "You two know each other?"

Mark replied curtly, "We've met."

"Briefly," Julie added.

"Perfect. I'll let you two work out all the details while I get back to work. Paperwork has been piling up all day," Mr. Owens held up his wounded hand with a chuckle.

Mark and Julie didn't say a word, each eying the other warily as they left the warm office. Once they were out the front door, Julie said, "I had no idea you were"—*young, good-looking, educated!*—"a teacher."

"Surprised that an old country bumpkin could have a college degree?"

"No, you just look different than I remember."

Mark was thinking that Julie looked different as well. If she wasn't such a city girl, Mark could almost think she was cute. Still he wondered about her little smile. *Getting a kick out of watching us hillbillies in action?*

There was an uncomfortable pause. "If you really don't want to go through with this, I'll understand," Julie said.

"Don't worry about it," Mark responded with a scowl. "I said

I'd do it, and I will. Unlike some people, I don't go back on my word."

Julie wondered what she had done to warrant that comment. She couldn't think of a thing, but decided to apologize anyway. "I'm sorry if I've done something offensive. I seem to have an irritating effect on you, and I don't know why."

She had an effect on him all right, but Mark wasn't about to admit what it was. In fact, the idea of giving the city girl driving lessons wasn't all bad. He'd like to see her squirm as he barked commands like a drill sergeant.

Glancing at the empty parking lot, he said, "Don't suppose you have a car?"

"Not yet."

Mark scratched his head. His old Jeep stood near the curb, but it was a temperamental old thing. "I'll see what I can round up."

"We can't use your Jeep?"

"It's a standard. You'll do better with an automatic."

"An automatic?" Julie wondered why he was talking about guns.

"You really don't know much about cars, do you?" When Julie shook her head, he pulled a manual from his briefcase and said, "Better study this then. When do you want to start?"

"The sooner the better."

"How about in the morning?" Mark taught the early session of driver's ed whenever possible. It got him out of the milking. "We could start at seven-thirty or eight."

After working all night, Julie knew she'd be dead tired at that time of day. She needed to be mentally alert for these lessons so she suggested, "How about afternoon? I'm asleep at eight."

"After school is fine," Mark replied with disdain. "Is three-thirty all right?" Julie nodded. "Good, until tomorrow then." He walked away. *Imagine being asleep at that time of day!* he thought. He wasn't sure he could spend the next week or two with such a lazy, spoiled-rotten city girl. He hoped this wasn't a mistake.

That thought was repeated the next afternoon as Mark checked his watch. It was ten minutes to four! He'd waited long enough. Kicking at a candy wrapper, he cursed under his breath, then headed for the Jeep.

Just then, Julie came careening around the corner on her bike, nearly colliding with a parked van and skidding into a stop in front of him. Her clothes were wrinkled, her hair was messy, and her makeup was smudged. She looked as if she had been asleep.

She had. After working all night, Julie had been unable to sleep earlier in the day. When she tried, she had dreams of guns, Jeeps, and endless fields of mud. She finally gave up and got dressed.

After a light lunch, Julie settled down on the couch to study the driving handbook Mark had given her. Soon she was fast asleep, only to wake up a few minutes ago. She literally flew to the high school.

"Sorry I'm late," she said breathlessly. "I overslept."

As he led her to the waiting car, Mark mumbled in irritation, "What kind of a person sleeps all afternoon?"

Julie didn't answer, too preoccupied by the sight of a red Honda at the curb. This was really it. Nerves finally overtook excitement. She brushed her hair back from her face and licked her dry lips. "Nice car."

After seeing Julie's bike riding, he hoped she wasn't that reckless behind the wheel. "It's my mother's car," he informed her. "She threatened my life if it got so much as one scratch on it."

"Oh," Julie started toward the passenger door, but Mark shook his head and escorted her to the driver's side.

"Nothing like jumping right in."

"I was afraid of that," Julie murmured. With cold, clammy hands, she gripped the steering wheel tightly. None of knobs or buttons before her matched the diagrams in the manual.

Mark slid into the passenger seat and, as an afterthought, fastened his seat belt. Then he explained, "You'll have to pass a written test and a driving test before you get your license. I'll get you through the driving part, but you'll have to study for the written exam. Did you read the manual?"

Julie nodded. She had read it, but didn't understand it. She had never paid much attention to the operation of motorized vehicles. They were simply a means to an end, a way to get from point A to point B.

"Let's go then," Mark said, accustomed to teaching teenagers who had been driving farm equipment for years. When Julie simply stared blankly at him, he shook his head and asked, "Do you know where the gear shift is?"

Julie shrugged lamely. She couldn't remember a thing she had read. Mark explained, in simple terms, all the basics. Her head was spinning too much to hear a word of it. Finally, he said, "Are you sure you read the book?"

Julie nodded, then put the car into gear as instructed. Mark braced himself for the inevitable peeling out. Most kids did it the first time. Julie, however, only inched forward.

"You can go a little faster," Mark prodded. When she didn't respond, he barked, "Push the gas pedal!"

She did, and worked her way up to a speedy ten miles an hour. Mark decided against a beginning drive to Antelope Flats. A trip around the block would suffice. At the speed they were going, it would probably take an hour. As they reached the corner, Mark directed her to turn right.

Julie's mind went blank. Right? *Right?*

"No, your other right," Mark yelled as she started to turn the wheel. They missed a fire hydrant on the corner by inches. Once they returned to the pavement, they proceeded at a snail's pace. Mark was about to make some snide remark when he looked over at Julie.

Her eyes were wide with fright, and she gripped the steering wheel with whitened knuckles. *She's really scared,* Mark thought. He reached over and patted her hand, "Relax. You're doing fine."

She wasn't, and she knew it. She would never get the hang of this. She forgot to signal, she almost ran over some kids, she was weaving all over the road. And no matter how hard she tried, she couldn't make the car go any faster.

Memories kept flashing through her mind . . . memories of working on accident victims at Mercy Hospital, memories of watching their loved ones suffer, memories of her own loss when she was eight years of age. She took this responsibility seriously since someone's recklessness in a car had cost her a family.

As they slowly circled the block, Mark continued his reassuring comments. Once he reached out with the intention of massaging the rigid muscles in her neck. As his hand brushed through her hair, Mark found it was as soft as it looked. He withdrew his hand quickly.

At last, they rounded the final corner. Both thought it was the longest ride of their lives! As they pulled into the parking lane in front of the high school, Julie applied the brakes firmly. Their stop was very abrupt.

Julie looked over to see Mark's head whipping forward sharply. Horrified, she exclaimed, "Are you okay?"

"Just a case of minor whiplash," Mark replied as he rubbed his neck. "I should be fine in a week or two."

With that, Julie burst into tears. Her nerves were shot. She would never get the hang of driving. She would never have true freedom. She'd be stuck on the bike forever. And to beat it all, Mark was actually being nice to her, and she returned his kindness by giving him whiplash.

Why did crying females always make him feel so inadequate? Mark wondered as he handed her a tissue from a box on the floor. "Hey, I was just joking about the whiplash."

Julie wasn't consoled. Between sobs, she managed, "I'll never get the hang of this."

"Sure you will."

"But I was so awful."

"I've seen worse."

"Really?"

"Definitely. You know, driving is like falling off a horse. The best way to handle it is to get right back on. Now dry those tears, hop back on that horse, and let's go around the block again."

"It isn't proper," Mrs. Ellsberg whined in a tone of conspiracy. "She comes and goes all hours of the day and night, you know."

Debbie was mending as her children played. She didn't invite Mrs. Ellsberg to join her on the bench. And she did little to encourage the gossiping, but the landlady persisted anyway. "She's supposed to be a Mormon, but I have yet to see her at church."

"Julie works on Sundays," Debbie defended her friend. "I've always thought it a shame that people still get sick on the Sabbath, don't you?"

Mrs. Ellsberg ignored that comment. She continued, "And the way she dresses! Well, I just hope she doesn't bring an unwanted element into our town. I was reluctant to rent to her, but Kathleen Ward insisted."

Debbie clenched her teeth. She could tolerate the landlady on most occasions, but today's unwarranted gossip was too much. She was trying to decide just how to tell her off when Julie rode past on her bike.

"Did you see how red her eyes were?" the landlady whispered. "She's probably on drugs or something. Keep an eye on her for me, will you?"

Mrs. Ellsberg scurried away as Julie walked over and slumped down on the bench next to Debbie. She ran her fingers through her hair and sighed. Debbie set her mending aside.

"What's wrong?"

"It was horrible!" Julie sighed deeply, then recounted the harrowing tale of her first try at driving.

"Is that all?" Debbie asked after Julie was done. "I thought it was something really bad."

"Making a complete fool of myself isn't bad enough?"

"Heck no! Now the first time I drove a car, that was something. The road was slick, and I drove right into a ditch."

Julie laughed. "That would be terrible. Makes my day sound like a picnic. Mark must really think I'm a mental case or something, though."

"Mark?"

"My driving instructor. He was so nice, and all I could do was cry."

"Not the same Mark you met in the corn field?"

"Yeah, one and the same."

"I thought he was a farmer."

"He is, but he also teaches at the high school."

"But I thought he was old and ornery."

"He isn't as old as I thought, and he was only mildly ornery. Hey, what were you and Mrs. Ellsberg talking about? She sure hurried away when I got here."

"That old biddy," was all Debbie would say.

By the end of the week, the driving lessons were progressing well. Julie knew the functions of all those knobs and buttons, as well as the rules of the road. She had even made it up to thirty miles an hour on the quiet, rural roads outside Oakwood.

Mark was a firm, but kind teacher. He was pleased with the progress she was making and had even fallen into a comfortable pattern of teasing her about driving so slow. He liked to watch her blush.

"You made it up to thirty-five today. That's a record," Mark commented on Friday afternoon before they parted at the end of their lesson. "Maybe we can make it to forty on Monday."

"Not tomorrow?" Julie was afraid she'd forget all she learned over the weekend.

Mark shook his head. He wasn't missed too much on the farm on weekdays. He had a lot of work to do, however, on the weekends. Just then, Mr. Owens walked out of the school. "How are those lessons?" he asked.

"Julie's doing well," Mark replied as the principal drew near, "except for that speed thing."

"A little speed demon, eh?"

"Something like that," Mark chuckled. Julie sent him an exasperated look, and he winked back.

Ignoring him, Julie turned to Mr. Owens. "How's your hand?"

"I get the stitches out this afternoon. Will you be there?"

"Not unless you come in at midnight."

"Well, count me out on that," he chuckled, then excused himself.

"You're a nurse?" Mark asked. When she nodded, he added, "And you work night shifts?"

"Temporarily, yes."

"I think I owe you an apology then," Mark looked sheepish. "All week I thought you were just incredibly lazy for sleeping all day."

"Oh that's all right," Julie laughed. "I've had a few unsavory thoughts about you this week, too."

Chapter Six

Julie was startled from a dozing stupor by three long beeps from the radio behind her. That was her signal. Setting the driving manual aside, she reached for the microphone to respond. A radio call was uncommon enough in Oakwood's emergency room, but on the night shift, it was downright rare.

"Oakwood Hospital," a voice crackled, "come in."

"Oakwood Hospital here, over," Julie replied, glancing at her watch. It was twenty minutes after three.

"Sheriff Porter, here. An ambulance is on its way. ETA, five minutes."

"What's the problem?" Julie never could remember the proper coded numbers. Checking a photocopied paper on the bulletin board, she said, "I mean, what's the 10-85?"

"We've got a young man here who's been stabbed."

"10-4. We'll be ready."

Sirens already wailed in the distance as Julie sprang into action. She assembled the necessary supplies with jittery hands. She'd cared for stabbing victims numerous times before, but never without the backup available at Mercy. There were no interns, no residents, and few other nurses here. Why, there weren't even dispatchers to answer the radio.

Offering a silent prayer for help, Julie paged the floating supervisor, Maggie. Then she checked the physician's on-call list. *Oh great,* she thought in disgust, *it's Dr. Poplin.* She cringed as she placed the call. He grumbled an incoherent reply to her report, and Julie hoped he wouldn't fall back asleep.

Just as she put down the phone, an ambulance screeched to a halt outside with lights flashing, followed by a police car. Two men in blue jackets wheeled an unconscious figure into the emergency room on a stretcher. A tall, thin policeman wearing glasses followed.

Julie rushed over and saw a young Indian with long black braids on the stretcher. *He's just a teenager,* she thought as she assessed him. His brown skin, cool and moist, appeared a few shades too pale. The bulky dressing on his stomach was soaked with blood.

Julie looked toward the EMTs. "Vital signs?"

"Blood pressure, 90/55. Pulse, 110 and thready. That's the second dressing he's soaked through since we found him, too."

Julie started an I.V. and let the fluid run in quickly. She took the young man's blood pressure 88/48 now. She taped a new dressing over the bleeding wound, securing it tightly with elastic tape. She put warm blankets over him and placed an oxygen mask over his face.

"Help me raise the foot of this stretcher," Julie requested of the man with a badge. "Sheriff Porter, I presume?"

"10-4," he answered, jumping up to help her.

"What's the story?" She checked the blood pressure again: 84/42. His pulse was 126 and weak. His respirations were shallow.

"His name is Woody Bluewhiskers. He's no troublemaker, but he was found behind a tavern on the south end of town tonight with a knife in his belly. No witnesses, or at least, none who will talk."

Julie felt a surge of anger. This wasn't fair. She hung another I.V. bag, then checked his eyes. Good. His pupils still reacted to the light. Maggie arrived to lend a hand as Julie drew a blood sample from his arm.

"I'll run a stat blood count on that," the supervisor said, then disappeared with the sample. Moments later, she returned and said, "Hematocrit, 23. His blood type is B negative, and I've got Sam doing a cross-match."

"Good," Julie replied with a smile. "He's going to need it."

The outside door opened, and Dr. Poplin entered with a flourish of arrogance. He immediately started barking orders for IV fluids, oxygen, and blood work, only to find that everything was already done. Dr. Poplin wasn't used to such initiative; it bruised his ego.

"We'll need to transport him to Logan," he announced after flipping through the chart. "Call in the ambulance crew."

"They're here," Julie nodded to the men in the corner.

"Humph! What did you call me for, young lady?"

Julie and Maggie exchanged exasperated glances. A tall, thin man brought in two bags of blood, and with the doctor's permission, Julie hung one on the I.V. pole. Dr. Poplin called a report down to the hospital in Logan as the ambulance crew loaded the boy back into the ambulance.

"You!" Dr. Poplin pointed to Julie before they closed the doors to the vehicle. "Ride in the ambulance and keep that young man alive."

Julie glanced at Maggie. "Go ahead," the supervisor said. "I'll watch things here."

Even with lights and sirens, it took over forty minutes to reach Logan. Julie worked and prayed all the way to keep young Woody Bluewhiskers alive. She didn't relax until she turned over his care to those at the larger hospital. All the way back to Oakwood, she slept in the back of the ambulance.

In the emergency room, she found Maggie at the desk. Sheriff Porter sat on a stretcher. The two were both grinning. They had just called Logan to find that Woody had made it through surgery and was listed in stable condition.

Sheriff Porter slapped Julie on the back. "You saved that kid's life tonight, Miss Craig. Good job."

Was that her mission in Oakwood? Could she move on now? Julie wondered about it as she rode her bike home. As she slept that morning, she had dreams of a large, unfinished puzzle. Only a few pieces were in place. She awoke, knowing her work here was not yet complete.

On Thursday, Mark and Julie sat in the Honda in front of the school, preparing for their final driving lesson. Having spent enough time on the road to meet the state's requirements, there was only one thing left to cover. Today was parallel parking day.

The afternoon was warm, and Mark tossed his jacket into the back seat. Rolling up his shirt sleeves, he settled in for the drive. Julie checked and double-checked all the knobs and buttons within reach before she turned the key.

She felt nervous—not only for parallel parking, but for the impending driving tests as well. She was scheduled to take both tomorrow. Mark insisted that she was ready, but she wasn't sure. Maybe another week or two of lessons. She wouldn't admit she hated to see them come to an end.

Mark's thoughts concurred, though he didn't acknowledge them either. Instead, he just scowled impatiently and said, "Let's go."

Just then someone walked up and banged on the back window. Julie jumped, and Mark snapped, "What the heck?"

He unrolled his window, and two teenage boys stuck their heads inside. One was blonde, the other had spiky brown hair. They grinned when they saw Julie in the driver's seat.

"Hey, Uncle Mark! We missed the bus. How about a ride home?" the blonde boy asked.

"Missed the bus? How did you two manage that?"

"Gary here walked Cynthia Benson home."

"And Troy tagged along with Misty Porter."

"Shhh!" Troy punched his friend in the ribs, then said to Mark, "You'd better not tell anyone! What about the ride?"

"You want a ride, and silence too?" Mark liked teasing his nephews. "Julie? Do you feel like playing taxi to a couple of lovesick boys?"

"Why not?" she replied.

As the boys climbed into the back of the car, Mark introduced Julie to his nephew, Troy Jackson, and his friend, Gary Carter. Through the rear view mirror, Julie smiled at them. Troy looked a lot like Mark, but younger and more carefree.

"With a beginner at the wheel," Mark warned, "you boys had better buckle up."

"Thanks a lot," Julie replied. "Now where are we headed?"

"Birch Creek," Mark announced. "Remember the way?"

Julie nodded, and they were off. As they went, Mark quizzed the boys on the final history test in his class tomorrow. Julie didn't join in, but concentrated on her driving.

Embarrassed when yet another car passed them by, Troy asked, "Why are we going so slow?"

Mark shot him a quelling look. "No back-seat driving!"

"But that was Gus Gledhill," his nephew complained.

"Quiet!"

Just beyond the road to Butterfield Basin, Mark directed Julie to turn right. A wrought-iron sign announcing Jackson Acres stretched over a graveled road. They passed some younger boys on bikes.

Julie noticed three houses—a brick house, an older frame house, and a small rambler—scattered between a mess of barns, sheds, and corrals. Julie noticed the Jeep sitting next to the rambler, and an old black dog on the step. *Did Mark live there?*

"Stop at the first house," Mark told her.

As the boys gathered up their books, Gary asked, "Hey, aren't you the new nurse?"

Julie had long since ceased to be amazed that everyone in this small town seemed to know everything about her. "That's me," she admitted.

"You saved Woody Bluewhiskers' life."

Julie answered modestly. "I just did what had to be done."

"Is he going to be okay?" Troy added.

"I called yesterday," she said. "He'll come home next week."

"Good," Mark said. Woody was a good student who was well liked by students and faculty alike, including Mark. "Now get out of here, guys. It's time for Julie's parallel parking lesson."

She moaned. "I was hoping you'd forget."

As they drove back across Antelope Flats, a dairy truck barrelled past them, followed by a Volkswagen bug. Julie tried to accelerate, but not before Mark started snickering, "You'd think a city girl would be burning up the pavement."

"I'm doing the best I can," she returned defensively.

"Pull over there," Mark pointed to a paved rest area where two trash cans were chained. "This should do."

"For what?" Julie wondered aloud.

"For parallel parking."

The trash cans looked awfully close together. "Are you sure?"

Mark assured her that he was very serious, then proceeded to instruct her on the mechanics of parallel parking. He even demonstrated, whipping the Honda between the trash cans with ease. After a dozen attempts, Julie managed to squeeze the car into the tiny space at a lopsided angle.

"Not bad," Mark remarked. "Now try again."

Julie tried a few more times. Finally, she did a decent job. She felt proud as Mark announced she was definitely ready for the driving tests.

"You'll need to practice a little before you drive in a city, though," he needled her. "I'd hate for you to create a traffic jam."

Mark always sounded sarcastic when he talked about cities, and it was starting to get on Julie's nerves. She tried not to take it personally, but it wasn't easy. As they returned to the highway, she asked, "What have you got against cities?"

A little taken back, Mark hedged, "Well, for one thing, I've never understood why anyone would want a million other people next door."

"Have you ever tried it?"

"Lived in a city all through college," he reported snidely. "You could go for days without seeing a living animal, except for flies and cockroaches. I couldn't wait to get back home."

"I know what you mean," Julie agreed. "Believe it or not, I felt like I'd come home at last when I came to Oakwood."

"Well, I can believe anyone wanting to leave city life behind. The noise, the traffic, the crowds, the trash. No, thank you!"

Julie looked at him. His fists were clenched, and a muscle in his cheek twitched madly. *His feelings about cities must run deep,* she decided. *Maybe something awful happened when he was there.*

"I can understand it if you had a bad experience," she conceded, "but you don't have to take it out on me."

Mark was startled from his thoughts by her comment. "Oh, have I been doing that?"

"I think so. I'm not to blame for your feelings, am I?"

"Of course not," Mark admitted. Nevertheless, the city was an old enemy of his. He had fought it once and lost. Never again!

Julie felt like she was walking on clouds as she left the sheriff's office the following morning. Even a fine drizzle of rain couldn't dampen her spirits. She held an umbrella in one hand and her temporary driver's license in the other. She had passed the test!

The sheriff himself had helped her. Upon spotting her in the office, he joked, "What are you doing here, young lady? Get a traffic ticket already?"

"I need to get my driver's license first," Julie laughed. "I'm taking the exams today."

"Well, here's the written one." He produced some papers from a file cabinet. When she returned it a while later, he looked it over, then handed it back to her with a grin. "You passed! Now if you can handle a car like you handle your emergency room, you'll be in good shape."

He ushered Julie outside for the second test. Even in the rain, she performed with confidence. When they were through, his only recommendation wasn't unexpected.

"Driving too slow," he said, "can be as hazardous as going too fast. Just try to go with the flow of traffic."

Even so, she received her license upon their return. She couldn't wait to tell someone. Debbie was gone for the weekend, and Vonda didn't answer her telephone. Neither did Stella. Julie just had to share her good news. Tucking the license into her pocket, she ventured back outside where the rain continued to fall.

The town was abuzz with activity that Friday afternoon. Of course! Julie remembered, it was the last day of school. Kids were everywhere, and a gigantic water fight was well underway in the middle of town, despite the rain.

Julie wandered over to the high school, wondering if Mark was there. Surely he'd like to hear about her license, wouldn't he? Spotting his Jeep in the parking lot, Julie ventured inside and inquired at the office about the whereabouts of his room.

The rain outside, the finals this morning, and the undisciplined mood of the students on the last day of school had given Mark a headache. He still had to clean up, count the returned books, and grade the finals. As much as the kids loved the last day of school, he hated it.

"Hey, guess what?"

He looked up from his work, thinking the interruption came from a student. When he saw Julie, he smiled. A pretty brunette was good therapy for a headache. He stood up to greet her. "Guess what, huh? You reached the speed limit?"

"No," she pulled out her license and waved it in the air. "I passed!"

"Great! I knew you could do it."

"Thanks to you!" Julie surprised him with a big bear hug.

Mark was caught off guard, but Julie danced back out of his arms before he had a chance to respond. She continued to wave the license, and Mark laughed. "I had no idea a slip of paper could be so exciting."

"It's not just a slip of paper," she grinned. "It's my freedom. Once I get a car, I can go places and explore things that I never could on my bike."

"And where's the first place you'll go?"

"Probably to Logan."

"Ah," Mark commented drily, "our nearest city, I see."

"You promised to lay off about that 'city' business," Julie reminded him. "I have some shopping to do."

"Shopping," Mark groaned. "It figures."

"I need some pottery supplies," she returned, "and I have a friend to visit in Logan, too."

"Who? Woody?"

"No, but maybe I'll visit him, too," Julie said with a smile. "Well, I hate to keep you from your work, but I just had to tell someone about my license. I'll see ya later."

She danced out the door, and Mark followed. He watched as she practically skipped down the hall. He'd have to tease her next time about being a kid at heart. What next time? He probably wouldn't be seeing her much after this. Faced with that possibility, he experienced an unexpected feeling of panic. He couldn't stop the words that came next.

"Would you like to go out?" he called out to her retreating figure. Where did that come from?! Lamely, he added, "To celebrate or something."

Julie stopped and looked back at him. A date? No—this would be a celebration. Without hesitation, she said, "Sure, I'd like that."

"What about. . . ." Mark thought a moment. Tonight was graduation. Not only did he have to attend, but he was chaperoning the all-night party afterwards. ". . . Tomorrow night? That is, if you don't have to work."

"It's my weekend off. The only thing I was going to do tomorrow was shop for a car. I'm not sure what I'm supposed to look for, though."

Thoughts of her at the mercy of a fast-talking salesman made Mark uneasy, especially when he thought of Oakwood's most notorious car salesman. "Why don't I go with you then?"

"Would you?" Julie smiled her gratitude. "I'd probably pick out a real lemon on my own."

Mark didn't doubt that one bit. "Pick you up at four? We can look at cars, then get some dinner or something."

"Sounds good to me. Let me give you the address."

Once Julie was gone, Mark returned to his classroom, finger-combing his hair and muttering under his breath. He hadn't been on a date for years. What was he getting himself into now?

Chapter Seven

Julie ruffled through her closet with a frown. Just exactly how did one dress to shop for cars *and* go out to dinner? Her black dress and pumps didn't seem appropriate for browsing through a car lot. But she couldn't wear jeans to dinner, could she? Stella would never allow it.

Stella . . . Julie looked through the latest care package from her aunt for help. There were three outfits inside—tight, white jeans with a fringed, white satin shirt, black leather pants with a matching leather jacket, and a shimmering nylon warm-up suit in hot pink and turquoise. They were Stella's idea of appropriate attire for Idaho.

The pile of discarded clothes on her bed grew until Julie heard a knock on the door. Oh, no! It was ten minutes to four! She hurriedly slipped on her robe, tying the belt as she dashed into the living room.

Cracking the door, she peeked out. It was Mark. Opening the door wide, she tugged self-consciously at the robe. "You're early."

"Sorry about that," Mark shifted nervously in the doorway. He wore tan slacks, a cream-colored polo shirt, and fresh-smelling aftershave. His cowboy boots were polished to a shine.

"Come in," she offered, "and I'll hurry."

Julie fled to her bedroom, discarded the robe, and threw on the first thing she found—a sleeveless red sweater and a denim skirt. She slipped into sandals as she fastened on red earrings. She grabbed her purse, stopped in the bathroom to check her makeup, then took a deep breath.

Ready or not, here I come, she thought as she returned to the living room. Mark, still on his feet, was studying a piece of her pottery. He appeared ill at ease as he looked over at her. "That looks better. I mean, you look nice."

"Thanks," she replied. After an uncomfortable pause, she added, "Do you like my pottery?"

"You made this?" Mark held up the piece in his hand. She nodded. "It's pretty."

"Thanks," Julie repeated modestly. "I'm not very good, but it's fun."

"Looks good to me," he set it back on the table. "Well, you ready to go buy a car?"

"Sure."

Mark escorted Julie by the elbow as they walked through the play area to the street. Julie noticed the curtains falling back into place as they passed Mrs. Ellsberg's window. That old busybody!

Once inside the Jeep, Julie recalled her first ride in it with a smile. My, how far she and Mark had progressed since their unfortunate meeting in the middle of the street. As Mark revved up the engine, he asked, "What are you smiling at?"

"Just wondering if you wanted me to drive," she teased.

"No way," Mark grinned back. "We don't have all night."

They rode to a car dealership on the south end of Main Street called Fast Eddie's New and Used Cars. His sign featured a race car driven by a voluptuous woman in scanty attire. The motto printed underneath read:

Welcome to Fast Eddie's . . .
Fast women and fast cars,
No matter how many you have,
There's room for more.

As she read it, Julie wrinkled up her nose in disgust. Mark knew that it was more than just a fancy motto. He still remembered all Eddie's locker room stories in high school. And if rumors were true, he hadn't improved much over the last ten years either.

"Eddie lives up to his name," Mark remarked dryly, "but there aren't too many choices in Oakwood. We can always go to Logan another day. Maybe sometime after next week. . . ."

Julie was impatient though. "Well, we might as well look around."

As Mark led Julie down the first row of cars, he commented, "I don't see many sports cars."

"Who's looking for a sports car?" Julie shrugged. "I've always pictured myself more as the station wagon type."

Mark nodded with surprised approval, but Eddie didn't have many station wagons either. In the end, it was a Ford Explorer that caught Julie's eye. She liked its rugged, outdoorsy look. It had four doors, an automatic transmission, and four-wheel drive. Mark said that would be useful this winter. Most of all, she loved the name—Explorer. It was perfect!

They were the only customers on the lot, but Fast Eddie didn't emerge from the office until they started looking over the window sticker. Then he sauntered over, smoothing back his hair as he did.

One word came to Julie's mind when she saw Fast Eddie: slick. His once blonde hair was slicked back, his three-piece suit was slick, and his actions seemed slick. Even his voice was slick; he was a regular smooth-talker.

"Long time, no see," Eddie pumped Mark's hand vigorously. "Your old Jeep finally give up the ghost?"

"Hardly," Mark nodded toward Julie. "I'm here with a friend."

Eddie's eyes widened with interest at the sight of a new girl in town. "Who's this beauty, Marko, old buddy?"

Reluctantly, Mark made the necessary introductions. When Eddie offered his hand, Julie responded likewise. Instead of the expected handshake, Eddie grasped her outstretched hand and held it to his lips. After an embarrassingly long time, Julie pulled her hand away, resisting the urge to wipe the offensive kiss off behind her back.

Mark instinctively put a protective arm around Julie's shoulder as he discussed options and warranties with Eddie. Julie didn't understand what they were saying, but she trusted Mark's judgment. She was glad he had accompanied her, especially when he finagled a test drive that excluded the obnoxious salesman.

"This isn't a bad vehicle," Mark announced after they returned to the car lot. He had put it through a series of maneuvers, the scariest for Julie being when he flipped on the four-wheel drive and bounced along a neglected dirt road for a couple of miles. Clinging to her seat for dear life, she was glad to see pavement again.

"You like it?" Julie asked hopefully. She had already fallen in love with it and wanted his approval.

"You could do worse," he admitted. "Paying cash?"

"I have enough for a down payment, but I'll need to borrow the rest."

"Don't finance it through Eddie then," Mark warned. The less she had to deal with him, the better. "See Mr. Standish at the bank and tell him I sent you over."

"Did you go to school with him, too?"

"No, but I taught his son last year. Putting up with that kid wasn't easy so he owes me one."

Fast Eddie was pleased when he heard that Julie wanted to buy the Explorer. He didn't even seem to mind when Mark kept himself situated between him and the girl as they dickered over the price. An agreement was reached, and they sealed it with a handshake. Julie would pick it up on Monday. They all shook hands before they parted.

"Are you sure I didn't need to leave a deposit?" Julie asked as they returned to the Jeep.

"Eddie is lucky if he sells one or two cars a month. Your Explorer will be there on Monday. Are you hungry yet?"

"Starved."

"Good."

They drove up Main Street, turned left at the traffic light, and went several blocks before stopping at a small restaurant across the street from a meat packing plant. "Willy's Grub" flashed off and on in red neon letters across the top of the building. Diesel trucks filled the parking lot.

"Willy's might not look like much," Mark commented as they walked inside, "but they have the best food in town."

"I love the atmosphere," Julie replied sincerely as she looked around. It was decorated with wagon wheels and pictures of cowboys. A large set of steer horns hung over the door, and the tables were covered with checkered oilcloths. The aroma of fresh bread hung heavy in the air.

Julie was glad she hadn't worn her black dress and pumps. Everyone at Willy's Grub wore jeans—even the waitress, who smacked her gum as she handed them a couple of menus and took them to a table. It was a booth in the back where a canning jar candle provided dim lighting.

Julie read the menu with a slight frown. Everything had a catchy name, and she wasn't sure what anything was. She was about to ask when Mark ordered for her.

"We'll have two Grub-busters. A Pepsi, and . . . ," he raised an eyebrow at Julie.

"A Diet Coke."

"Coke?" Mark asked after the waitress left. "How can you drink that stuff? It's so sweet."

"I suppose Pepsi is better?"

"Of course."

Their conversation continued casually until the waitress returned with two huge steaks. Each was so big that it covered the entire platter. The accompanying potatoes, corn, and homemade bread were served on separate plates. Julie stared dumbfounded at the slab of meat, still sizzling before her.

"Are they serious? A person is really supposed to eat all this?"

"You said you were hungry."

"I am. I slept through both breakfast and lunch today," she remarked. She picked up her utensils and cut into the steak. "It looks like a good thing I did."

"Still working night shifts?"

"Yes, but only for a few more days. I'll be on day shifts soon, and I can't wait."

"I don't know how you get used to it," Mark stifled a yawn. "I was up all night myself. I tried to sleep in this morning, but I still feel groggy."

"Up all night?"

"I chaperoned the big party after graduation last night."

"Sounds like fun."

"Riding herd over a hundred or so wild-eyed, hormone-crazed graduates isn't exactly fun. Every year I swear I'm not going to do it again."

"But you do?"

"Yeah. It's one of the hazards of being a single teacher. I can't say 'no' and blame it on my wife," he commented dryly. "How's your steak?"

"Delicious."

And it was. She was surprised that she ate as much as she did. Even so, she still had a large piece left as she held her stomach and moaned.

"Need a doggie bag?" Mark asked her. When Julie shook her head, he added, "I'll take your meat then. Old Max will love it."

"A dog, I assume."

Mark nodded, tucking a generous tip under his empty glass. A few minutes later, they were sitting outside the restaurant in the Jeep. Neither was anxious to call it a night. Mark was trying to think of something else to do when she said, "I can't get enough of these stars. They're so incredibly big and bright."

"If you think these are great," Mark looked up at the dusky sky, "hold on, and I'll really show you something."

He pulled out of the parking lot with a grin, and Julie recognized their route until they passed the Jackson farm. Then the road became increasingly more winding. Several miles later, they drove past a small church, then up a dark lane behind it. They circled around and stopped at the top of a hill, the lights of the valley stretched out beneath them.

"Where are we?" Julie asked.

Mark answered matter-of-factly, "In a cemetery."

Sure enough, she saw headstones in the shadows beyond their headlights. All of a sudden, Julie hoped Mark wasn't some kind of pervert. When a coyote yapped in the distance, she shivered in the cool night air, spooked by the sound.

Mark noticed. He reached behind the seat and pulled out an old leather jacket. As he slipped it over her shoulders, an aroma of musty leather, sweat, and faint after-shave encircled her. Her voice quivered as she thanked him.

"Does it bother you to be here?" It had just occurred to Mark that his intentions could be misconstrued.

"A little."

"Sorry. I wouldn't have brought you, except the view is so spectacular." He leaned over and switched off the headlights.

Julie gasped as a million stars immediately filled the dark sky. Without a moon, their numbers grew by the minute, their twinkling unchallenged. Julie leaned back in her seat and stared upward in silence for a few minutes. "This really is something. It makes me feel so small, so insignificant," she said in a reverent whisper.

"I know," Mark answered in an equally quiet tone. "I used to spend hours here with my grandpa. He knew all the constellations. There's the Big Dipper."

"Where?"

"See that bright star up north? Right next to it, the stars make a big pan with a crooked handle. See it?"

"Yeah! Where's the Little Dipper?"

"Well, it's harder to find."

"Show me!"

With their heads leaning close together—as close as the

bucket seats of the Jeep would allow—Mark pointed out all the constellations he knew: Cassiopeia, Draco, Cepheus. "That one is supposed to be a king, but Grandpa West always called it 'the great outhouse.'"

"This is incredible! You'd never see this in the city."

"How well I know," Mark returned. "Still like country life, do ya?"

Julie smiled contentedly. "Oh, yes! It's so peaceful. We're in Birch Creek, right?"

"You betcha, and you should see this in the daylight. It's like you're on the top of the world."

"I'd love to. The road grew too steep for me and my poor little bike."

"Yeah, right," Mark laughed, doubting much could slow Julie down if she really set her mind to it.

They stared at the stars in silence a few more minutes. Feeling very much a part of the universe, the creation, and the eternal plan of salvation, Julie said softly, "Do you ever wonder where heaven is?"

The atmosphere between them, so friendly moments ago, cooled considerably. Mark pulled away from her. "Not really."

Julie wondered what she had said this time. Was religion a sore subject with Mark, like big cities? She had assumed that he was a Mormon—almost everyone in the valley was. Now, she wasn't sure. Cautiously, she asked, "Are you LDS?"

After a long pause, he growled, "I guess you could say that."

"I don't understand."

Mark's voice was strained, "I grew up in the Church, but I haven't been back for years. You aren't a Mormon, are you?"

"As a matter of fact, I am. I was baptized last October," Julie replied. Noticing his scowl, she added, "Does that bother you?"

"Well, I guess not. I just didn't know they had any Mormons in New York. I mean, I guess I figured you were safe."

"Safe?"

"Just don't start preaching to me," he snapped.

"The thought hadn't occurred to me," Julie assured him, wondering why he was suddenly so defensive. "Freedom to believe, or even not to believe, is a constitutional right. Surely a history teacher like you would know that."

"Whatever," he muttered. But the peaceful mood of the evening had been shattered, so he started up the Jeep. "It's late. I'd better get you home."

As they drove back into Oakwood, the conversation was strained. Julie was afraid of saying something that would be considered preachy. Mark was wondering why everyone had to be so gung-ho about the Church. Neither were speaking at all by the time they walked to her door.

"Let's do this again sometime," Mark commented without conviction.

"Any time," Julie answered too brightly.

He nodded and headed back towards the Jeep. Julie sighed as she closed the door behind her. It wasn't until she heard him drive off that she realized his leather jacket was still on her shoulders.

The next day was Julie's first opportunity to attend church in Oakwood. Dressed in a suit of gray that matched the overcast sky and her mood, Julie walked to church alone since Debbie was gone for the weekend. She hoped that she would fit in in her new ward.

As she mingled a little in the foyer, then took a seat in the chapel, Julie felt . . . well, disappointed. It wasn't the ward members' fault. She couldn't quit thinking about the abrupt end to her date last night. Would she see Mark again? Did she want to?

During sacrament meeting, Julie noticed Mrs. Ellsberg among the congregation, though the latter didn't acknowledge her. It was a missionary farewell, and the bishop, who didn't conduct, stood to give a few remarks at the end of the program. When he did, Julie smiled. It was Mr. Owens!

After the meeting, he pulled her aside in the hall before

Sunday School class and shook her hand warmly. "Julie! It's nice to see you here. We just received your membership records from New York this week. I wondered if you'd ever get away from that hospital long enough to join us."

"I'll come when I can. By the way, how's the hand?"

He stretched his fingers, "Good as new! Did you get your driver's license all right?"

"Just Friday, and I'm buying a car tomorrow."

"Good for you. Now I have a favor to ask of you."

"Anything."

"We like to hear from the new members of our ward in sacrament. Can we schedule you for the third Sunday in June?"

"Talk? In church? What on earth could I talk about?"

"Your conversion story would be interesting. We don't get too many new converts in Oakwood."

Julie knew she should do what was asked of her. And Bishop Owens had arranged her driving lessons. She put her hesitation aside and agreed. She had three weeks to prepare, but she felt the butterflies settle in already.

"Preachin' at church?" Vonda asked later that night as they spoke on the telephone. "What kind of a fool crazy idea is that?"

"Well, we don't have paid clergy. In fact, the high school principal is the bishop of our congregation."

"Then why doesn't he preach?"

"He asked me to talk. Everyone takes turns."

"You, a preacher? What kind of church you got there, child? I've been to church all my life, but I ain't never heard of the likes of that."

As Julie wrote in her journal later, she glanced back through the front of the volume. She had started writing it on the day of her baptism. Would these Mormons, members all their lives, really be interested in her conversion? She couldn't imagine it making a difference to any of them.

Chapter Eight

On the following Thursday, Julie drove into Logan alone. With maps spread out beside her, she followed the road signs carefully. She even reached forty-five miles an hour before the winding canyon road caused her to slow down again.

Even so, she had never enjoyed a ride so thoroughly in her life. Country music played on the radio, a cool breeze teased her hair, and a feeling of well-being enveloped her. The Explorer was really hers!

Mr. Standish at the bank had laughed when Julie asked why he owed Mark Jackson a favor. He pointed to the distinguished sprinkling of gray at his temples and said, "That child of mine is responsible for this!"

He turned the loan over without a fuss. Julie wished she could say the same about getting the car keys from Fast Eddie. He literally chased her around the desk as she signed the papers. She sincerely hoped to never see him again.

The trouble was worth it, though. In her spare time, she had travelled from one end of Pine Valley to the other. The trip to Logan was her first adventure beyond it. Once in Cache Valley, she followed the temple on the hill like a beacon and drove straight to Mrs. Parsons' house.

After a lengthy visit in her cozy parlor, Julie decided to head back home. She had never driven after dark. Before they parted, Mrs. Parsons reminded her of the birthday party at the end of the month. Once again, Julie agreed to attend.

Near the outskirts of Logan, Julie saw the hospital's sign. On a whim, she decided to check on Woody. She didn't really know him, but felt a kinship after their brief encounter in the emergency room.

Julie peered into Woody's room to see him lying in bed. With only pajama bottoms on, a large white dressing on his abdomen contrasted sharply with his dark skin. His hair, pulled back at the nape of his neck, was snarled from what Vonda always called "bed head."

A middle-aged nurse stood at his side, her ample bosom shaking as she spoke, "You are going nowhere, young man!"

"The doctor said I could," he insisted firmly.

"Your mother can't arrange a ride until tomorrow."

"Hi," Julie entered the room with a bright smile. "You must be Woody Bluewhiskers."

Woody scowled at Julie. He'd seen too many doctors, nurses, dieticians, social workers, and therapists lately to greet another newcomer with any civility. The buxom nurse also seemed suspicious. "Can we help you?" Her eyes narrowed as she stared at Julie.

"I'm the nurse who treated Woody in Oakwood."

Woody nodded in her direction with dignity. The nurse busied herself at the sink, so Julie filled the silence. "I was in Logan today so I stopped by to see if you were mending."

"I'm well enough to go home," he glared at the other nurse, "but she won't let me go."

"You don't have a ride," his nemesis reminded him.

"I'll walk then."

"I'm going back to Oakwood," Julie offered. "Want to come with me?"

"Could I?"

"Sure."

"Let me check on that." The nurse seemed as relieved as Woody.

She left the room, and while they waited for her return, Julie told Woody about the night in the emergency room. He listened quietly, then asked a single question, "Do they know why I was attacked?"

Julie shook her head. The nurse returned with the paperwork for Woody's release. Twenty minutes later, they were on the road to Pine Valley.

As they went, the miles passed quickly once they hit upon Woody's favorite topic—sports. He was a track star, and had won a couple of races right before the stabbing. He hoped this wouldn't slow him down. Julie thought he'd be fine when track season started again next spring.

They reached Oakwood just before dark. When they stopped at the stoplight, Woody offered to walk from there.

"Didn't they tell you to take it easy?" Julie scolded.

"Yeah, but. . . ."

"But nothing. Tell me where your house is, or we stay put."

The light turned green and someone honked. Woody finally gave her directions. She drove through a rough section of town to a rundown trailer court, stopping beside the third trailer on the left. It was ancient, but clean.

They were met at the door by a middle-aged woman. She wore a satin blouse of rich blue, a long black skirt, and beaded moccasins on her feet. Her thick hair was pulled into a figure-eight, held in place by a beaded, leather barrette.

Woody introduced her as his mother, then spoke to her in their native tongue. Mrs. Bluewhiskers smiled shyly at Julie. She reached for a fringed bag at her side that jingled with coins.

"Oh no!" Julie exclaimed with a shake of her head. "I couldn't possibly take money for the ride. Please tell your mother it was my pleasure, Woody."

Woody did, and his mother nodded solemnly, turned, and walked back into the house. Julie hoped she hadn't offended Mrs. Bluewhiskers. Later that evening, she discussed it with Debbie.

"Don't worry about it," her friend advised, wrapping a towel around little Brandy. "I'm no expert, but all the Indians I've met are quiet."

"But she just walked into the house without a word."

"You worry too much about offending people."

"I can't help it. I'm a nurse. It's my job to worry about others."

"At least you'll know what to do when you develop an ulcer," Debbie laughed. "Sometimes you just have to do what is right. If people are offended, that's their problem."

Julie wondered about Mark. Had she offended him by defending the Church? He hadn't called, not that she expected him to, but still, she had his jacket. His number wasn't listed, or she would have called him herself—about the jacket, of course.

As she struggled to diaper her wiggling child, Debbie added, "I have only two more words to say on the subject, Julie. Quit your worrying!"

"That's three words."

"Whatever, just do it."

Julie was glad when her shift was over on Monday. Day shift was definitely busier than nights. A steady flow of patients passed through the emergency room doors all day. Some had been sent from medical offices for x-rays or lab tests. Others had minor complaints, few had true emergencies.

Returning to her apartment, she found a package on the doorstep. It was small, wrapped in newspaper, and tied with a white string. Her name was written on the front in pencil. It wasn't from Stella. Julie was sure of that.

Julie went inside, found some scissors in a kitchen drawer, and cut the string. Two items—a leather barrette like Mrs. Bluewhiskers' and a pair of leather moccasins, also covered with elaborate beadwork—and a note fell out. Julie reached for the note with a puzzled smile.

> *Dear Miss Craig,*
>
> *We hope you will accept these gifts. My mother apologizes. She didn't realize that money would offend you. The hair piece is her way to thank you for driving me home. The*

moccasins are my way of thanking you for saving my life. I hope they will express what I feel in my heart.

Woody Bluewhiskers

The gifts were too much, Julie thought. She slipped on the moccasins and ran her finger gently over the smooth beading, touched to think they had worried about offending her. She wasn't sure if she wanted to laugh or cry.

Someone knocked on the door, and Julie quickly wiped tears from her eyes, then removed the moccasins before answering it. It was Mark, grubby as ever in muddy boots, work clothes, and his cowboy hat. Without his friendly smile, he would have looked just like "that ornery, old farmer" of the past.

"Looks like you got the Explorer all right," he said without preamble, nodding in the direction of her parking stall.

"Without a hitch," she smiled.

"I hope Eddie behaved himself."

"Well, I didn't have to slap his face," Julie joked, not mentioning that she was awfully tempted to. "Please come in. You must be here for the jacket."

Mark looked puzzled. "What jacket?"

"The one you loaned me last week. I'm sorry I forgot to return it after our ride."

"Oh, yeah. I wondered where it went."

Julie went to the bedroom to get it. She breathed in its masculine aroma one last time before she returned to the living room and handed it over. Mark threw it casually over his shoulder. "Thanks."

"But if you didn't come for the jacket," Julie inquired, "then why?"

"Can't I make a social call?"

"Sure," she replied, "but after the other night, I thought you'd be steering clear of a Mormon girl like me."

"Sorry about that," Mark smiled weakly. "I think I was just

tired."

"That's all right." Julie glanced again at Mark's attire. "Looks like you've been busy on the farm today."

"The tractor's been on the blink all week, and Steve couldn't get it going while I was gone."

"You were gone?"

"Chaperoning the senior class trip. Just got back last night."

That explains why he didn't call, Julie thought with glee as she asked, "Where did you go?"

"Up to Yellowstone."

"Yellowstone! Really? I'll bet it's beautiful."

"Not with a school bus full of kids!" Mark shuddered. "Listen, I wondered if you wanted to go for a horseback ride sometime this week. I'm checking fence lines and could use the company."

He wanted to see her again! For some reason that make her want to turn cartwheels. Instead, she replied, "I'd love to."

Julie met Mark at Jackson Acres, and they drove up to Rick Lee's ranch together. Rick was gone, but he left horses for them in the corral. One was a bay mare, the other a buckskin gelding, Mark explained as he deftly saddled them, then helped her into the saddle of her horse.

"Little Al is a good horse," Mark said as he swung onto his own mount. "She knows what to do, so let her do the work."

"She? A female named Al?"

"Well, her real name is Annie Laurie," Mark explained. "When Rick married Annie, she didn't want a horse with her same name, so they started calling her Little Al. The horse, not the wife. Ready to go?"

They crossed the highway eastward and rode through green pastureland. Julie soon grew accustomed to the rhythm of the mare's stride. She held the reins as Mark instructed and even tried giving the appropriate signals. When Little Al responded, she was pleased.

Following a series of dirt trails, they checked fences. Mark pointed out that the land once belonged to his Grandpa West.

Pioneer ancestors homesteaded it in the late 1860s, he explained, building a log cabin where the farmhouse now stood. Both the house and the farm slowly grew until they had reached their current spread.

The land now belonged to Mark's mother. When her parents passed away, her siblings were scattered across the west. They were willing to take a cash settlement for their inheritance, but Mark convinced his mother to take the land for her share.

With that and Jackson Acres, they had more land than Steve could farm, even with Mark's help. So they leased Grandpa West's land. Mark said that his mother was always talking about selling, but this time, she even hired an appraiser. That's why they were checking fences now. Old Gus never quite got around to fixing them.

Julie noticed the tightness in Mark's voice as he spoke of the upcoming survey and possible sale. She could see why. This part of Birch Creek was different than the area around the Jackson farm. The mountains were closer, more striking. The creek sparkled in the sunlight, and the air was fresh with the aroma of mountain grass.

The sun was high overhead when Mark suggested, "How about lunch?"

"Good idea," Julie replied.

"Not a very good spot for a picnic, is it?" Mark admitted, looking at the loose rock and scruffy-looking brush that surrounded them. "I know where we can go, though. Follow me."

They climbed up a hillside, crossed a canal on a rickety-looking bridge, then slipped into a wooded area. Riding through quaking aspens and pines, Mark talked about camping there with Rick when they were young. They used horses, dirt bikes, and snowmobiles to explore and conquer.

Julie was mesmerized by the serenity of her surroundings. To have such a place in one's backyard was a marvel. The forest floor, carpeted with a thick layer of decaying leaves, crunched beneath the horse's hooves. A bird warbled in the distance. A squirrel scampered across their path.

Fording a small stream, they joined a trail that went straight up the side of a mountain. Julie was glad for a good old horse like Little Al. Her main concern was to stay in the saddle.

At last, the trail leveled off. It continued on to their right, and a little dell appeared on the left. Quiet and secluded, it was surrounded on three sides by rocky slopes covered with pines. A small, clear stream tumbled over the rocks through thick, mountain grass.

"Does this look better for a picnic?" Mark reined to a stop.

"It's . . . it's wonderful," Julie whispered in awe.

"If you think this is great," Mark pointed to where the trail continued upward, "you ought to see it from the top."

"The top of what? Where are we, anyway?"

"On the back side of Angel's Peak."

"Angel's Peak?" she asked. "Isn't that the big mountain we saw from down by your grandfather's farm?"

"One and the same," Mark replied with uncharacteristic animation. "It's probably my favorite place in the whole world. You should climb it sometime."

"I'd like to." Julie smiled at his enthusiasm.

He dismounted, and Julie climbed awkwardly down herself before he could help her. Her legs felt so shaky when she tried to take a step that she decided to stay where she was. Mark laughed as he tethered the horses near the stream.

Retrieving a saddlebag, he warned, "You'd better keep moving."

Julie groaned. "That's easy for you to say."

"Your muscles will freeze up if you don't," Mark replied knowingly. "In fact, be sure to go for a walk tonight, then soak in a hot bath."

"You sound like a nurse."

"How many first-time horseback riders have you treated?"

Good point, she conceded, trying to comply with his advice. She walked around stiffly while he unpacked their lunch and spread it out on a fallen log. Mark sat down, inviting Julie to join him in the dappled sunlight.

She limped over, dropping the gloves he had given her on the ground before she pulled a baseball cap, also compliments of Mark, off her head. As she ran fingers through her sweaty hair, the insignia on the cap, a red bird holding a baseball bat superimposed by an intertwined "STL," caught her attention. "St. Louis Cardinals?"

"You bet," Mark answered as he handed her a slightly smashed sandwich from the saddlebag.

"You went to college there?"

"Naw." Mark looked off into the distance with a frown.

"Why the Cardinals then?" Julie prodded.

"Well, when I was twelve, my dad took me with him to a livestock show in St. Louis. We went to a couple of Cardinal games. They played the Chicago Cubs and swept the series. It was great. I've kept an eye on them ever since."

"Your dad is a farmer?"

"He was," Mark said quietly. "St. Louis was the last happy memory I have of him. He died later that summer."

"I'm sorry," Julie said with understanding. Losing a parent was never easy, she well knew.

Mark continued pensively, "My brother, Steve, took over the farm. It was a struggle for a while, but Jackson Acres is doing fine now."

They ate in silence for a few minutes, washing down their food with water from the canteen. The horses flicked at flies with their tails, and a bee buzzed lazily over a patch of dainty, purple wildflowers.

"We'd better get back," Mark said at last, rising to his feet. "As it is, you're going to be a little sore."

"A little?" Julie said through clenched teeth as she struggled to her feet.

"Need help?"

"Sure, but be careful. You don't need a hernia."

"A hernia?" He lifted Julie back into the saddle with ease. "Why, you're no heavier than a sack of hog feed!"

Was that a compliment? As they returned down the mountainside, she was once again thankful for the sure steps of Little Al. They made it to flat ground in one piece, then rode side by side. Julie felt sore, but contented.

"Oh, guess what?" she said, remembering some news she had wanted to share with Mark. "They finally pieced together what happened to Woody the night he was stabbed."

"It's about time," he replied. "So what's the scoop?"

"It seems Woody was walking home from a late track meet. He ran into a couple of drunken patrons near the tavern. They saw red—literally—and jumped him. Apparently, one of them lost his job a few days earlier, and the foreman hired an Indian to replace him."

"So Woody was in the wrong place at the wrong time?"

"Apparently so. And three to one, he didn't have a chance. He's lucky he didn't bleed to death before someone found him."

"Well, I hope they're rotting in jail now."

"They're out on bail, awaiting trial."

Mark scowled up at the sky for a moment, then hissed, "Damn, stinking drunks! They ought to be shot."

Julie was startled by his harshness. Why was Mark so moody? He could tease and laugh as well as anyone, but some topics triggered his ire . . . like cities, the Church, and now drunks. He must have had some hurtful experiences in his life.

She wanted to reach out and erase those deeply etched frown lines. Vonda would call it her caregiver personality, which was common among nurses. They wanted to fix everything. There were some pains, though, that a shot or a pill couldn't cure. Was there anything she could do for Mark?

Chapter Nine

Over the next few weeks, Julie quit worrying about why she was in Oakwood and simply enjoyed life in the country. She drove the Explorer whenever possible, but to keep in shape, she tried to ride her ten-speed once in a while as well. In spare moments, she worked on her pottery.

On her days off from work, she took blood pressures at the senior citizen's center. Fast Eddie stopped by, complaining that she made his blood pressure rise, but she turned him away for being too young. She visited with Debbie often, talked with Vonda on the phone nearly every day, and received another care package from Stella.

Julie saw Mark a couple of times, too. One evening they went to dinner at a little Mexican restaurant called Conchita's. Another time, they drove over to Preston to watch Troy play baseball. Woody watched from the bleachers and waved when he spotted them. He looked good, Julie thought.

They even went on a few more horseback rides, one of them through Snow Canyon. As they rode past the headwaters of Birch Creek, Julie was amazed at how the icy water sprang right out from under a gray wall of rock. Each ride left her less and less sore when she dismounted.

As Julie's relationship with Little Al grew, so did her friendship with Mark. They teased, they laughed, they talked. As long as she didn't mention life in the city, the Church, or alcohol, things were fine.

Neither wanted anything more than friendship. Mark was glad for an excuse to get out of the house, but he was scared of relationships. And after living with Stella, dating Vinny, and enduring Vinny's mother all those years, Julie liked running her own life for a change.

The Saturday before her scheduled talk in church, she and Mark drove to Logan. They ate at Fredrico's, a pizza parlor east of the university. It was crowded, but not like Angelo's in New York, Julie thought with a smile. They went to a movie at the mall afterwards.

It was dark when they returned to the Explorer. Julie had offered it for the trip, but Mark insisted on driving. They needed to get back home before dawn, he teased as they hit the road.

They talked for a while, then the conversation lagged, but the ensuing silence was a comfortable one. The Oakridge Boys were on the radio, and the passing scenery was awash in soft moonlight. Suddenly, Julie let out a long sigh and shook her hands out as if they had been asleep.

Mark asked, "Something wrong?"

"Nerves, I guess."

"Nerves?" He turned down the radio. "How come?"

"I have to give a talk in church tomorrow. Oh, I wish it was over."

Mark nodded with understanding. He hadn't given a talk in years, but he remembered the experience. The words, so easy when he practiced, always stuck in his throat at the pulpit. If it wasn't for Grandma West, smiling up at him from the front row, he'd have never made it through.

"Find a friendly face in the congregation," he advised, "and talk directly to them. You'll do fine."

"Sounds reasonable," Julie agreed without conviction, "but that's just the problem. I won't know anyone there."

"What about your friend—Debbie, isn't it? Isn't she in your ward?"

"Yeah, but her brother's missionary farewell is tomorrow in Malad."

"You don't know anyone else?"

"Well," Julie thought a moment, "there's Mrs. Ellsberg, but I don't think she counts."

"Lavon Ellsberg?" Mark sounded amazed. "She's still around?"

"She's my landlady," Julie answered glumly.

"She used to be our substitute teacher in grade school. Never could take a joke, though. What a sourpuss!"

"I can imagine. Focusing on her face would be no comfort at all."

"You're probably right about that," Mark agreed. "Anyone else?"

"Well, Mr. Owens is my bishop," she admitted.

"There you go," Mark said brightly. "You know him. He can be your friendly face."

"But he'll be sitting behind me. I can't very well give my talk with my back to the congregation," Julie sighed. "Oh, well . . ."

Mark was touched by the sound of desolation in her voice. He wanted to help, but how? A thought came to him, but Mark quickly dismissed it. It cropped up again. He tried to dismiss it again. After a few minutes of silent wrestling within, he knew what he had to do.

"What time does your sacrament meeting start?"

"Quarter to eleven."

"And you go to that pink brick church on Main Street?"

"Yeah. Why?"

"Thought I'd come down and let you focus on my face." Mark tried to sound nonchalant, but he felt like he was going to the guillotine.

Surprised, Julie started to protest, "But you don't . . ."

"Isn't my face friendly enough for you?" Mark snapped lightheartedly. This wasn't easy, and he didn't want to make a big deal out of it.

"Of course it is," Julie reached over and gave his arm a little squeeze. She knew this was a sacrifice for him. "Thank you, Mark. It means a lot to me, really."

"Glad to be of service," Mark put a free hand over Julie's. He hadn't felt this good in years. Now if he could just survive the church meeting.

Sarah Jackson slipped away from church a little early the next morning to put a roast into the oven. Her son Mark had called earlier to say he was bringing a guest to dinner. She didn't mind. There was always room for one more at her table.

Mark always came over for Sunday dinner, as did Steve and his family. Their sister Robyn came down from Evanston whenever possible. Neighbors, friends, extended family all were welcome. It had been years, though, she thought as she scrubbed potatoes at the sink, since Mark invited anyone.

Sarah glanced out the window and was shocked to see him leave his house in Sunday clothes. She watched him climb into his Jeep and drive off in the direction of Oakwood. What on earth?

Sarah didn't meddle much in her children's business. After all, they were adults and could live their own lives. She had raised them to be good kids, even if they sometimes strayed a little. And Mark was having a struggle in his life right now.

Even so, Sarah could think of only one reason he would be all dressed up on a Sunday. He had to be going to church. Could it be true? Was her youngest mending his ways? She could only hope and pray.

Mark slipped into the chapel during the opening song. He hadn't been inside a church for more than five years. He looked around, deciding sourly that things hadn't changed much. The congregation was as pious-looking as any other.

The room was warm, and everyone seemed restless. Children were fussing, the boys on the back row were snickering and shoving, the widows were gossiping in loud whispers. Mark ran a finger under his shirt collar. *I hope Julie appreciates this!* he thought. When he caught her eye, the relief evident in her smile appeased him. Just this once, he could endure for her sake.

As the meeting progressed, memories tugged at Mark. His actions were automatic. He had never missed church as a child. During his teen years, though, religion had taken a back seat to friends. In college, he had studied on Sundays, attending church only when it was convenient. When he returned, work on the farm became his excuse.

Lukewarm, that was a good word to describe his attitude toward the Church. He was lukewarm. Well, up until about five years ago, that is. The bitterness he now harbored didn't come until after the accident.

During the sacrament song, he focused on the words, "I stand all amazed . . . a soul so rebellious and proud as mine . . . that for me, a sinner . . . his great love unto such as I."

They touched him. Seeds of testimony, planted years ago and allowed to lie dormant since, started the faintest stirring of life. Did the Savior really love him? Especially after all these years? Feeling uneasy, Mark leaned over with his head in his hands until Julie's name was announced.

As Julie approached the pulpit, she was certain that she was going to be sick. Her mouth was dry, her palms hot and sweaty. Her knees threatened to buckle beneath her, and her heart was pounding in her ears. When she spotted Mark, he winked at her.

She smiled back weakly, took a deep breath, and began, "Talking in church is a new experience for me, so I asked Debbie Ventura for advice. She said to keep it short, and I'd be a success."

A soft laugh rumbled through the congregation. Focusing on Mark, Julie continued, "I was asked to tell you about my conversion to the Church. That happened last October, but the story began long before.

"I was raised in a suburb in upstate New York, the only child of loving parents. We attended church almost every Sunday, and it was there I learned right from wrong. I learned about Jesus and memorized the ten commandments in Bible class.

"When I was eight, my world was shattered. My parents died unexpectedly, and I was shipped to New York City to live with an aunt. She wasn't used to children, so she left the greater part of my upbringing to the nuns at parochial school.

"The nuns didn't like all my questions. I didn't like their vague answers. I wanted to know where my parents were, and if I would ever see them again. They chastised me for lacking faith, but never satisfied my curiosity.

"Eventually I quit asking, graduated, then studied nursing. I wanted to save lives, perhaps to make up for those taken from me as a child. I did save some, but lost a few, too. When that happened, the nuns at Mercy Hospital had no better answers than the others. I cried with the grief-stricken families.

"Other than that, though, I didn't think much about religion. I had a career, a steady relationship, money, clothes, friends. I had an ideal life, and yet something was missing. It felt like a large hole that neither money nor friends could fill.

"I thought it was because I lacked family. Memories of my parents were like a hazy dream . . . you know, that warm, fuzzy feeling that fades when you wake up. Just when I gave up ever seeing them again, I met a pair of Mormon missionaries with a message of love and hope to share.

"During the discussions, Brother and Sister Montague had all the answers to my questions. I would be reunited with my parents again, and we could be an eternal family forever. Death wasn't forever! What sweet music that was to my lonely ears.

"The decision to be baptized was easy for me, but not for those around me. My friends faded away, my boyfriend gave me an ultimatum, and my aunt thought I was crazy. She still does. Only one friend supported me. She respected my decision and even came to my baptism.

"Through it all, one thing stands firm in my heart. I have been led by the Spirit to make the right decisions. I know the Church is true. I love the Savior. I'm thankful He sent the Montagues to New York to teach me the gospel. Baptism was definitely the right decision.

"I know that moving to Oakwood was also the right thing to

do. I'm not sure why I'm here, but the Lord sent me. And I pray that He will guide my path to find and fulfill my purpose, my mission here, faithfully."

Julie ended her talk and sat down. Glancing at the clock on the wall above the organ, she couldn't believe she talked so long. She hoped it sounded all right. When Mark gave her a thumbs-up signal from the congregation, she sighed with relief.

After a rest song, Bishop Owens spoke briefly on missionary work. He invited all the young men to serve and advised the young women to pray about it as well. He told the older couples that, like the Montagues, they could be valuable assets in the mission field. He encouraged all to be missionaries by example in their daily lives.

After the meeting, Mark waited for Julie in the foyer. It took a few minutes for her to reach him, but when she did, he chuckled, "Good job, young lady. And you had such doubts."

She grinned. "I'm glad it's over anyway."

Before they could leave, Bishop Owens came over to shake Julie's hand. He was as surprised as anyone to see Mark, whose negative attitude towards the Church was a well-known fact throughout the community. Bishop Owens shook his hand vigorously, "How's the summer been treating you?"

"Not bad, and you?"

"There's trouble brewing up in Boise, I hear. Something about the legislature cutting funding for education."

"Well, let's hope they can work it out before fall," Mark replied, feeling a little uncomfortable. He turned to Julie, "Ready to go?"

Julie was aglow with happiness as they drove to Birch Creek. It felt like the day she got her driver's license. She had tackled something difficult and won. She reviewed her talk mentally more than once, and was pleased with it each time.

Mark couldn't quit thinking about the things she said either. Finally, he said, "I'm sorry about your parents."

"Death is never easy, but we adjust, right?"

Julie was thinking about the death of Mark's father, so she wasn't surprised when he muttered, "Yeah, death's a bitch. Oh, sorry."

"That's all right," she returned softly.

Talk turned to other things, like Julie's aunt and her friend, Vonda. Never had Julie talked so openly about her past.

By the time they pulled into Jackson Acres, though, Mark still hadn't broached the one subject utmost on his mind, the results of her boyfriend's ultimatum.

Instead, he said, "If you were an only child, I hope all the family togetherness you're about to experience isn't too overwhelming."

Julie didn't understand until they entered the oldest of the three houses. There were boys, funny papers, Nintendo games, dogs, and noise everywhere. Two women scurried around the kitchen while a man sat at the table, reading the sports section.

Mark cleared his throat, and everyone froze. The older of the women quickly turned off the television, scooped up scattered newspapers, and then rushed over to greet them with a hug. Mark introduced her as his mother, then presented the rest of the clan.

"You're just in time for dinner," Sarah said warmly, leading Julie to a large, oval table in the kitchen. It was covered with a white linen cloth, and a small vase of flowers from the garden served as a centerpiece. The pattern on the china was worn and faded, but all the silverware matched.

Chaos continued as the meal commenced. Everyone grabbed serving dishes at random. Food was passed to the left and the right, and everyone talked at once. Julie finally quit trying to follow the conversation and just observed the lively bunch instead.

Sarah Jackson seemed down-to-earth, smiling often as she eyed Julie with curiosity. Steve was an older, heavier version of Mark, and his wife, Joyce, was equally plump. Their three boys, all eating with gusto, held the family resemblance with blonde hair and blue eyes.

Julie remembered Troy, and she noticed Tommy trying hard to follow in his footsteps. Little Thad held her interest the longest, however. His short hair stuck up stubbornly in the back, and he had a mess of freckles on his face and arms. His two front teeth were missing, causing a healthy lisp. What a doll! No wonder Mark talked about him so often.

When the meal was over, Joyce had each boy tell what he had learned at church that day. Troy mumbled something about tithing, and Tommy told the story of Solomon's temple. Thad learned a Mr. Clean trick.

"When you have a bad thought," he lisped with enthusiasm, "just th'ing your favorite Primary th'ong and the bad thoughts di'th'appear. Hey, Uncle Mark, what did you learn in church today, huh?"

"Thad!"

"Well, he's in his Th'unday clothes, isn't he?"

"Thad!"

The admonishments came from his mother, but the whole Jackson family was horrified. They knew better than to mention church to Mark. Last time they did, he stomped off and wouldn't talk to any of them for days.

"That's okay," Mark laughed good-naturedly, knowing he was wrapped around Thad's little finger. "As a matter of fact, I did go to church."

Silence fell over the table. Sarah was secretly ecstatic while Steve and Joyce were stunned. Troy looked at Mark like he was some kind of traitor, and Tommy's mouth hung open. Thad, however, remained undaunted.

"How come I didn't th'ee you there?"

"I went with Julie in Oakwood," Mark explained to his youngest nephew, "to listen to her talk in sacrament meeting."

"How come?"

"So she'd have a friendly face to look at."

Thad thought a minute, then a huge grin spread across his face. "Come with me next week then, 'cuz I need your friendly face for my talk in Primary."

What could Mark say? Especially with the whole family waiting for his answer and Little Thad looking at him like that. When he agreed to go, everyone looked at their plates and no one dared say a word.

As the conversation returned to normal, Mark turned to Julie and muttered, "Now look what you've gotten me into."

Julie simply smiled. The words of Bishop Owens, spoken earlier that day, echoed through her mind. Thad was being the best kind of missionary, both innocent and unyielding!

Chapter Ten

Mark experienced déjà vu as he slipped into Birch Creek's church the next Sunday. If he had planned it right, he'd be just in time for Thad's talk. Then he could sneak back out before anyone saw him, Mark decided as he entered the Primary room.

When he saw his uncle, Thad waved wildly. Mark returned the greeting with a little smile, glad that no one else acknowledged his arrival. Even Joyce and Sarah, seated just in front of him, didn't seem to notice.

When his turn came, Thad marched right up to the miniature pulpit. He gave his talk word for word, just like he had practiced it all week. Mark found himself smiling and holding his breath at the same time.

Thad didn't return to his chair when he was done. Instead, he ran straight to Mark and hugged him tightly around the legs. With that, everyone turned and stared, including his mother and grandmother. So much for slipping away unnoticed, Mark thought with a frown.

His plans were further foiled when he ran into several neighbors as he left the building. They all stopped in their tracks, stumbling over their words to greet him. Mark was cordial, but brief, escaping as soon as possible.

Outside, Rick Lee was sitting under a giant willow tree, teaching a class of deacons. Upon seeing Mark, he stopped in mid-sentence. He flashed a questioning look at his friend, but Mark ducked into the Jeep with a shrug.

Mark felt better once he pulled off his tie. Instead of heading back to the farm, he drove up to the quiet cemetery. *If only . . .* he lamented, *if only things had worked out differently.* He could have been listening to his own child's Primary talk.

Wishing hadn't changed anything yet, Mark thought as he drove home. Even so, he was restless for the remainder of the morning. Chores were done, so he stayed in his good clothes. He tried reading the paper, but mostly wandered around the empty house. The silence was deafening.

He wandered outside and fed old Max. It was too quiet out there as well. Sunday dinner had been canceled since everyone was having a big family get-together that evening in Logan. Mark cooked a frozen meat pie, but it made an unsatisfying meal.

He finally drove into Oakwood, but Julie wasn't home. *Oh, yeah,* he thought, *she had to work.* Thad had invited her to be a friendly face, too, but she had declined. With nothing better to do, he drove over to the hospital. He hoped Julie wouldn't mind.

She was wrapping white gauze around a teenaged girl's arm. "The burn isn't bad. Keep the ointment on it for a few more days," he heard her say.

He was once again impressed by Julie's caring manner. She truly seemed to care about everything and everyone. That was one of the reasons Mark liked being with her. How long had it been since he had cared about anything? Five years, that's how long!

As the girl's mother left to get the car, Julie went the other way to wash her hands. The teenager looked up and saw Mark. "Hi, Mr. Jackson. What are you doing here?"

"Just visiting."

Julie spun around and smiled. What a pleasant surprise! And she hoped that the way he was dressed, nice slacks and a striped dress shirt, meant he'd made it to Thad's talk. Eyeing the two of them, the girl giggled as she walked out the door.

When they were alone, Julie said, "I hope this isn't an official visit."

"No, just bored."

"So, tell me, how was Thad's talk?"

"Great! Looks like you survived our bowling game last night."

Julie smiled, "Still upset that I won?"

"I never was upset. And I'm not a sore loser, either." Mark looked around the empty emergency room. "Busy day?"

"No," she rubbed on some hand lotion. "In fact, that was my first official visit of the day."

"You have many unofficial ones, besides me?"

"Only one. That car salesman."

"Eddie?" Mark snapped irritably. "What did he want?"

"He said he'd die of a broken heart if I refused to go out with him."

"And what did you say?" Mark managed through clenched teeth.

"I told him I'd come to his funeral."

Mark relaxed. Julie could take care of herself. Glancing at his watch, he asked, "You're almost done here, aren't you?"

"Yeah, why? Don't tell me you want to go bowling again?"

"On Sunday? Why, Miss Craig, I'm shocked! Seriously, we're having a huge family party in Logan tonight, and I know how you like the family torture thing so I wondered if you wanted to go."

"I wish I could," Julie answered sincerely, "but I have a birthday party to attend tonight. Did you say your party's in Logan? Maybe we could drive down together, at least."

"Better than nothing," Mark shrugged, trying not to be disappointed. The get-together would have been easier to handle with Julie at his side.

"Want to take my Explorer?"

"If I get to drive."

They left for Logan after Julie freshened up. As they went, they made plans to spend the Fourth of July together. They would climb Angel's Peak in the morning, then attend the annual dutch oven dinner in Birch Creek that evening. Julie thought it sounded like hometown fun.

Their plans now were for Mark to drop Julie off at her birthday party, then return in an hour or so to pick her up. He'd use any excuse to leave his own party early. As they reached the outskirts of Logan, he asked, "Now what was that address again?"

Julie read it from her organizer, and then added a few directions. Why was Mark laughing? She didn't say anything funny. Between chuckles, he asked, "How old is your friend anyway?"

"Eighty-something, I can't remember exactly."

"Her name wouldn't happen to be Emma Parsons, would it?"

"Why, yes! How did you know?"

"She's my grandmother!"

"Your grandmother? But how?"

"My father's mother."

"But her name isn't Jackson."

"She's outlived three husbands so far," Mark explained.

As it finally clicked, Julie laughed. "So your get-together is a birthday party for your grandmother?"

"Yeah," Mark nodded. "Looks like we're headed to the same party."

The birthday celebration was as crowded as Mark predicted. Julie lost track of him not long after they got there. She was in the care of Sarah, though, who seemed determined to introduce her to everyone in the house.

She met close relatives, distant relatives, neighbors, and friends. She met Mrs. Parsons' daughters, each as talkative as their mother. She met Mark's sister, Robyn, seven months pregnant with her second child.

The noise was unbelievable . . . people laughing, singing, arguing, and talking at the top of their lungs. When the meal was ready, the throng moved to the backyard where the noise level rose, as if it were possible. Julie found Mark there, playing tag football with his nephews. Mrs. Parsons was there, too, crawling around to measure her next croquet shot.

Mark joined Julie for the blessing on the food. She brushed some grass off his sleeve, then he guided her by the elbow to the table of food. Before they reached it, they were waylaid by Mrs. Parsons, who put an arm around each of them.

"So you've met, huh? I hoped you would. Would have arranged it myself, but I know how you hate meddling, Mark."

He just rolled his eyes. They filled their plates, then sat on the grass to eat. After the last steak was grilled and the last scoop of potato salad served, it was time for Mrs. Parsons to open the gifts.

"I said no presents this year," she scolded, but looked pleased all the same. She exclaimed with delight as she opened each one, even the booklet of knitting patterns Julie brought. "Oh, I love it! How thoughtful, dear."

As Mrs. Parsons dawdled over her birthday gifts, Julie slipped inside to find a bathroom. When she was finished, she wandered through the quiet house for a moment, rubbing her temples. Mark was right; his family possessed both volume and enthusiasm.

In the empty parlor, she paused to look at the photographs, a favorite pastime of hers. The faces were almost like friends. She browsed slowly now, then stopped short.

Those deep, blue eyes of the young high school graduate. She knew those eyes. They were Mark's eyes. Why hadn't she noticed before? Her gaze darted to the wedding picture of the same young man. That had to be Mark, too! Married? But who? How? When?!

"He was young, wasn't he?" Mrs. Parsons whispered, slipping an arm through Julie's. "Got married straight out of high school, but it was a poor match. Oh, the heartaches that boy has suffered."

"Grandma!" Mark, who had apparently followed his grandmother inside, bellowed from the doorway, "Julie doesn't need to know about that." He turned and stomped out, slamming the front door behind him.

Julie was confused, not only about the picture and what it

meant, but about Mark's sharp reaction to her discovery of it. She looked from the door to Mrs. Parsons and stammered, "I don't understand!"

"No time to explain," her elderly friend scurried her out the door behind Mark. "Go after him."

Julie didn't see that she had much choice. The whole thing was making her head spin, but Mark had her keys in his pocket, and she'd miss her ride if she didn't catch him. She slipped into the vehicle seconds before he peeled out.

"My Explorer isn't used to such speed," she said lightly as they raced down the street. Mark didn't answer, but slowed ever so slightly. Julie made several more attempts to lighten the strained atmosphere, but failed. Finally they drove in silence.

Right before they reached the end of the canyon, Mark pulled into a graveled rest area. Lights twinkled below them, but neither enjoyed the view. Mark was scowling, and Julie sighed, wishing she knew what to say.

After a long silence, Mark said, "Did Grandma tell you about my divorce?"

"No," Julie replied quietly. "She didn't really have a chance to tell me much of anything. It's funny, though. I've looked at those pictures for weeks now, never realizing they were you."

"That bad-looking of a kid, huh?" Mark tried to joke, but his heart just wasn't into it. He stared blankly out the window. "I bet you think I'm a real jerk."

"For stomping out of the party, or for being divorced?"

"Either, both."

"Well, there are worse things than divorce." Julie thought of the bruises Vonda had to hide before her husband died. "One of them is being married to the wrong person. It happens."

"Not around Oakwood, it doesn't. People can't understand that I made a mistake, an awfully dumb mistake when I was too young to know better."

"Haven't we all made mistakes?" Julie paused. "Want to talk about it?"

"It isn't easy. I haven't talked about my . . . my ex-wife since she left."

Julie sensed his anger as well as his sadness. "You loved her, then?"

"I thought I did. Maybe it was infatuation because by the end, all my feelings for her were gone."

There was another pause. "If you want to talk about it . . .," Julie offered again.

"You really want to hear this ancient history?"

"I wouldn't mind. Besides, it would be a good way to put the past behind you."

"Maybe you're right," Mark sighed. "Well, we met at the rodeo the summer before my senior year. Rick and I felt pretty cool when some girls from Logan started chasing us. We got their telephone numbers, then flipped a coin later to decide which one we should each call. I got Denise.

"We started dating. A long-distance romance was hot stuff, and we thought we were in love. I ran up a terrible phone bill, and Ma kept harping about it. It made me want to call Denise all the more.

"About then, everyone was pressuring me about a mission, too. I didn't see any reason to go, just because every other male member of my family back to the pioneers did. So I rebelled. Man, I really rebelled.

"When I asked Denise to marry me, Ma was fit to be tied. Grandma begged me to see the light. Steve took me aside for a few father-son talks, but he wasn't my father, so I didn't listen. In fact, the more they talked, the more determined I was to get out of there.

"Pretty soon, Denise and I couldn't agree on anything. I wanted to get married in Birch Creek, but she insisted upon Logan. I wanted a small wedding, she wanted a fancy affair. It wasn't worth a fight, so I went along with whatever she wanted.

"Actually, I went along with a lot of things. I wanted to go to college in Logan, but Denise refused. She wanted to see the world. I ended up in Los Angeles. I hated it, but Denise didn't. She thrived on the glamour.

"We lived in a tiny apartment, but that wasn't a problem for Denise. She was never home. I went to class, studied, then did most the housework when I got home. When we were together, we fought. I wanted her to be a regular wife. She wanted to 'get out and live.'

"I sent out only one application when I got my teaching degree, to Oakwood High School. When they hired me, Denise was furious. She threatened to stay behind, but in the end, she came with me. She hated it here though, hated every minute of it.

"We stayed together two and a half more years. At first, we tried to get along. But in the end, we quit even trying. When the last reason for us to stay together was gone, she left. Not a word, not a note, nothing. A year later, I got a lawyer. I never regretted signing those divorce papers either."

Through it all, Mark spoke in a monotone, as if stripping his voice of emotion would lessen the pain in his heart. Julie noticed and hurt for him. Her voice quivered as she whispered, "I can't even imagine. Do you ever see her now?"

"Denise? No, she hightailed back to the city as fast as she could. Last I heard she was in Chicago, but that was several years ago."

No wonder Mark hated the city so, she thought as she rested a hand upon his shoulder. "Do you miss her?"

"No, not really," Mark took her hand and squeezed it. "Actually, I don't miss her at all. It was a mistake, and I've been paying for it ever since."

"Alimony?"

"No, just emotionally."

"I hope you don't mind me saying this," Julie spoke openly, "but it sounds like you made the right decision."

"I wasn't guided by the Spirit or anything," he claimed sarcastically, remembering her sacrament meeting talk.

"Sometimes the Spirit whispers, even when we aren't listening."

He didn't speak for a few minutes. When he did, it was to ask, "Now you know about my past, still want to spend the Fourth of July with me?"

"If you think this is an excuse to back out," she cuffed him lightly on the chin, "think again, buster!"

"Okay, okay!" Mark held up his hands in mock defeat.

After work on Friday, Debbie and Julie went to buy farm fresh eggs. Debbie claimed that they made all her recipes taste that much better. On the return trip, Cody wiggled out of his seatbelt, reporting the more interesting things he saw out the window to Brandy, who was snug in her carseat.

"Wook, Bratty, a cow," he said with excitement. "Moo, Moo, MOOOOO!"

"Sit down," Debbie snapped at Cody. She turned back to Julie. "Are you sure it's okay? It will be like a second honeymoon to get away with Chip, even for one night."

"Wook, Bratty, a lambie. Baa, Baa, BAAAAAA!"

"We'll be fine," Julie assured her friend. "After all, I'm a nurse. Besides, what could possibly go wrong?"

"I appreciate this, really. Let me know if something comes up this week. I'll understand if you can't tend."

"Wook, Bratty, a puddytat. Meow, Meow, MEOOWWW!"

Unfortunately, Debbie didn't see the cat steal across the road. A loud thump heralded the last of its nine lives. She pulled over, and Julie got out to survey the damages. The cat was clearly dead.

"Yucky, huh Jewsy?" Cody yelled out the open window. "What's dat squeaky sound?"

Julie heard it, too. She followed the noise to side of the road where two tiny puffs of kitten fur huddled in the grass. One was gray, the other white with black spots. Julie gathered them up into her arms.

"That must have been their mother." Julie nodded toward the

mangled heap in the middle of the road as she walked towards Debbie.

"Oh, that makes me feel better," Debbie said with exasperation.

"Hey, a baby puddytat!" Cody cried. He held out his chubby hands. "I wanna puddytat."

"No," his mother replied as Julie walked over and let him choose one. He picked the black and white one. When she saw how he cuddled it in his arms, Debbie repeated herself. "No!"

"But they're so small," Julie protested as she snuggled the shivering gray one up to her cheek. Kittens were a part of her life in the suburbs, a part she had to give up in the city. "They'll never survive out here."

"My puddytat name Spot," Cody announced.

"Cody Ventura, don't you dare get attached to that kitten."

"Spot wanna go home, Mama."

"Bubbles the goldfish will feel bad if you bring another pet home."

"Bubba wanna friend."

Debbie knew she was losing ground. She had only one argument left. "Mrs. Ellsberg doesn't allow pets. You know that!"

"Spot loves me, Mama. He does. Him belly is singin'."

"Julie, help me out here." Debbie started up the car. "Don't you have anything to add?"

Julie was as eager to keep her kitten as Cody was to keep his. "Let's just make sure Mrs. Ellsberg doesn't find out."

Chapter Eleven

Julie spoiled her kitten rotten that night. She fed it warm milk, let it sleep in her bed, and couldn't wait to get a toy mouse for it. Since it was nearly the Fourth of July, she named it Uncle Sam.

Saturday morning dawned bright and beautiful. Dressed for hiking, Julie packed another outfit for the picnic that evening in a bag, then tucked Uncle Sam inside, too. He had a happy reunion with Spot at Debbie's place.

As planned, Julie met Mark at eight. From Jackson Acres, they drove to the base of Angel's Peak and parked in a clearing littered with empty beer bottles. After donning a knapsack, canteen, and a pair of binoculars each, they were ready to hike.

Mark led the way. First they crossed a creek by jumping from rock to rock. Then the trail headed straight up. Julie recognized it as the same trail they took that first time on the horses. And as she huffed and puffed, she thought, *Where's Little Al when I need her?*

At last, they reached the shady dell. As Julie drank from the canteen, Mark assured her, "The rest isn't nearly as steep, I promise."

Julie wiped her mouth with the back of her hand. "Steep or not, it's sure pretty up here."

Beyond the dell, the trail zigzagged up the side of the mountain in a series of switchbacks. Mark found a knobby shaft of wood for Julie to use as a walking stick, then pointed out tiny fossils in the rock along the way. Their shouts at Echo Point were answered again and again. Before long, they were scrambling over cactus-covered rocks to the summit.

The view from the summit amazed Julie. "Oh, wow! I can't believe this!"

They had a bird's-eye view of Birch Creek in miniature wonder below. There was the creek, the cemetery, and the church. There was Jackson Acres, Rick's ranch, and Grandpa West's farm. There was the ballpark where people were already preparing for the picnic.

Through binoculars, she could see Butterfield Basin across the valley to the west. To the south, she caught a glimpse of Oakwood behind rolling hills of green. To the north, Bear Lake glimmered beyond Snow Canyon. To the east, pine-covered mountains stretched forever.

Mark watched her reaction. "You really like it up here?"

"Like it?" she returned with wonder. "I love it!"

"Unbelievable." His voice was snide.

Julie was irked at his tone. "Believe it or not, I love this country life. I'm not Denise, you know."

Julie wanted to retract the words the moment she said them, but Mark only sighed. "How well I know it. She'd be too busy complaining to even notice the view."

Julie wondered if he still cared about Denise. She made a point of keeping the conversation light as they descended the peak, but he still seemed distracted. By the time they reached the farm, however, things were back to normal.

Mark's house, Julie decided, looked like the bachelor's pad it was. The lawn needed to be mowed, and the siding needed paint. Inside, the sink was full of dishes. The only plant in sight was a dead fern on the fridge, the only wall hanging a dusty St. Louis Cardinals pendant.

She changed her clothes first, then yielded the bathroom to Mark. A little embarrassed when she heard him run the shower, she went outside. When he was dressed, he found her sitting on the back step, scratching old Max's head.

"You do that very long," Mark warned, "you'll have a friend for life."

"One can't have too many friends," Julie returned with a grin. "Hey, you look good. That light blue really sets off your eyes."

"Flattery will get you everywhere," Mark replied, looking down at his new denim shirt. Then reaching over to ruffle her hair, he added, "You clean up pretty good yourself, kid."

"Who you calling a kid?"

They joked all the way to the ballpark. Any tension left from their hike was gone. Once they arrived, however, it was strictly business. Sarah was in charge, and she was running the picnic like a boot camp.

"Go over to the fire pit, Mark," she commanded, "and Julie, I could use you at the serving table."

Julie was assigned to put a roll on each plate. A million or so rolls later, she was finally rewarded with a plate of her own. Soon it was heaped with mutton, dutch-oven potatoes, corn on the cob, green salad, Jello, watermelon, pie, and her very own roll.

Mark sat beside her at one of the long tables. Moments later, they were joined by another couple. The man sported a dark mustache, and the woman was slightly overweight. They both eyed Julie with interest.

"Hey, old buddy," the guy greeted Mark by swiping his hat, "I thought you were allergic to social gatherings like this."

"I am, but Sergeant Sarah has spoken. Julie, meet Annie Lee. And this old thing she has to put up with is Rick."

Julie had heard a lot about them from Mark. She could easily see why he liked them as they joked throughout the meal.

At one point in the conversation, Annie pointed to Mark's arm. "Hey, Mark, what's that welt on your arm? A love bite?"

"Hardly," Mark sent her a withering look.

"Let me see," Julie demanded, prodding at the fresh wound with a fingertip. He didn't even flinch. "Doesn't that hurt?"

"Naw," he shrugged, "it was just a little spark from the fire."

"Little? It's the size of a quarter, and it's blistering. That's a second-degree burn, buster."

"Like they say," Rick teased, "no brain, no pain."

"Oh, yeah?"

"Yeah. Remember when you broke your arm and didn't even know it for a week? Proves my theory, right?"

"Theory, schmeory," Mark retorted, trying once again to free his arm from Julie's grasp. He only succeeded after promising to buy and use burn ointment. *Being friends with a nurse,* he decided, *sure can be a nuisance.* On the other hand, it was nice to have someone worrying about him again.

After the meal, Rick and Annie went to find their children while Julie and Mark wandered over to a grassy slope. For such a small community, the fireworks display that followed was surprisingly long. With each brilliant burst, spectators uttered ooh's and aah's in unison.

Before the grand finale, a voice crackled over a bullhorn, "Hey, folks! You know what time it is!"

Mark pulled Julie to her feet. As the final explosions of light filled the sky in rapid succession, an old and slightly crazy Birch Creek tradition commenced. Hugs and kisses of celebration spread throughout the crowd, reminding Julie of Times Square on New Year's Eve.

Unexpectedly, Mark grabbed her and planted a kiss upon her lips. It was brief, but oh, so sweet. When it was over, neither said a word. Both felt weak in the knees. Both wondered why their hearts pounded so. Both contemplated the frightening possibilities that single act unfolded.

And both hoped no one saw them. Someone had, though, and she was overwrought at the sight. LuAnn Frost—thirty, homely, and single—had always figured poor Mark was hers for the taking. But seeing him kiss another woman? Well, she could certainly handle a little competition.

Julie was exhausted before she even began her stint of babysitting a week later. All three stretchers in the emergency room, as well as several chairs at the desk, were occupied after an automobile accident. By three o'clock, she was both physically and emotionally drained.

The sky was overcast as she drove home. Too tired to shower or even eat, she changed her clothes, then went over to Debbie's. Uncle Sam went along, hidden under her shirt.

Julie was greeted by an enthusiastic bear-hug from both children. She admired their energy and hoped, with a yawn, she was up to the challenge ahead. Debbie rattled off a list of last-minute instructions while Chip put their suitcases into the eighteen-wheeler.

Julie and the children waved from the curb as the truck pulled away. Once it was out of sight, Brandy took one look at Julie and burst into tears, while Cody took off running after his vanishing parents. With a writhing child under each arm, Julie staggered inside.

It was all downhill from there. Julie tried to read stories to them, but she kept dozing off. After one particularly long blink of the eye, she awoke with a start. Where were the children?

Crash! Julie jumped to her feet, nearly tripping over Brandy, who was nestled in the middle of a huge pile of books. The bookshelf she ran past was completely bare. And Cody? Julie ran to the kitchen, where a dozen broken eggs oozed across the floor.

"Wanna make cookies, Jewsy?" Cody asked innocently.

He had bowls and flour everywhere. Julie found Debbie's recipe, smudged from frequent use, and tried to put together a batch. The lumpy things that resulted didn't resemble any cookie she'd ever seen. Cody took one look at them and abandoned the project.

Crash! Julie followed the sound into the children's bedroom. The baby's crib was tipped over, and the mattress was off Cody's bed. Every toy was out of the closet, and every piece of clothing was out of their drawers. Both children sat happily in the middle of it all, putting together a puzzle.

The telephone rang, and Julie answered it in the kitchen. Before she could convince the salesman that she didn't need light bulbs, Cody had to go to the bathroom quick! They made it just in time, and Julie rewarded him with a piece of bubble gum.

Julie glanced at her watch and sighed. Five-thirty. Would she survive the next eighteen hours? Would the children? A blood-curdling scream sent her back to the bedroom. Cody was trying to pull his bubble gum out of Brandy's hair. Julie gritted her teeth and snipped off a few of the baby's long-awaited curls.

Crash! Off to the kitchen she flew, only to find Cody on his hands and knees, lapping milk from a saucer with the kittens. Figuring he was hungry, she ordered pizza.

It arrived two long, harrowing hours later. She handed the box to Cody while she rummaged through her purse. By the time she had paid, Brandy was covered with strings of cheese and sauce. Cody's cheeks bulged as he chewed on three pieces at once.

Julie sighed as she took a piece herself. "I guess this means baths."

She was hoping to avoid that. Five minutes later, Cody appeared, fully dressed and soaking wet. His hair was plastered to his head with lotion, and a ring of blue toothpaste encircled his mouth like a clown's grin.

"I baffed, Jewsy. I'm a d'ood helper, huh?"

"Very good," Julie agreed with forced patience.

"Bubba take a baff, too."

Julie shuddered, not even wanting to know the poor goldfish's whereabouts. The doorbell rang. Now what? She harbored half a notion to ignore it, but Cody skipped right over and answered it. When Mark stepped inside, Julie flew to him.

Mark was both surprised and pleased at the welcome. "If I'd known I was getting that sort of a greeting, I'd have been here hours ago," he said as he held her tight.

Julie couldn't answer. She was too close to tears. She hid her face in his jacket, her lips quivering as she fought to regain her composure. Cody and Brandy simply stared from the kitchen door.

Finally, Julie pulled away from the embrace. "I . . . I thought you were hauling hay tonight."

"I was," he looked around, "but we're done, so I thought I'd see if you needed a hand."

"Oh, we're getting along fine," Julie lied, unwilling to admit she was out-matched by a couple of kids.

"What's this?" Mark lifted a piece of cheese from her cheek. "The latest in facial masks?"

"So we made a little mess," Julie brushed flour from her pants, "but we had fun doing it. Haven't we, kids?"

The children nodded solemnly. Just then a flash of lightning outside was followed by a loud clap of thunder. They both burst into tears. Even Julie looked a little spooked. She turned to Mark with an embarrassed grin. "If you want to stay, though, that's fine with us."

"No problem." Mark closed the door behind him with a smile. "After all, what are friends for?"

Friends? Vonda! Oh dear! She was expecting a call from Julie tonight. She'd send out the FBI if it didn't come. Frantically, Julie asked, "What time is it?"

"Eight-thirty. Why?"

"I need to call New York. Would you mind if I ran home a minute? I hate to run up Debbie's bill."

"I think I can handle that."

It took Julie almost an hour to get up the nerve to return to Debbie's. She hoped Mark wasn't too irritated with her for taking advantage of him. She needed the break, though. She probably had enough energy now to put the children to bed, then tackle the mess no, messes.

When she walked in, Mark was slipping the last book into the bookshelf. Freshly scrubbed children sat in pajamas on the sofa, watching cartoons. Bubbles swam happily around his bowl atop the television. The miracles weren't confined to the living room either.

"You did this?" Julie asked incredulously. "Amazing!"

"Not really," he shrugged. "One two-year-old is about the same as another."

Julie thought of how lively Thad could be and laughed. With a tone of authority, Mark announced it was time for bed, and the children were soon tucked in. Julie kissed them each goodnight, but before the lights were turned off, Cody said, "Help me say mine prayers, Mawk."

Mark looked helplessly to Julie, but she just shrugged. Once Cody made up his mind, there was no changing it. With resignation, Mark knelt and helped him bless everyone they knew, including Spot and Uncle Sam.

Before the adults could make it to the hall, a clap of thunder shook the apartment. Julie couldn't help but jump. From the darkness, Cody advised, "Don't worry, Jewsy. Funder's just clouds bangin' toget'r, huh, Mawk?"

"Sure enough," Mark answered, "now get to sleep."

In the living room, another flash of lightning brought a look of alarm to Julie's face. Mark gave up the notion of leaving just yet and led her to the sofa. As the storm raged on, she sat stiffly by his side, fidgeting with each explosion of its wild fury.

"Don't you have thunderstorms in New York?" he teased, trying to erase her anguish.

"Yes, we do," Julie answered quietly. "It was storming like this the night my parents died. I will never forget that."

Suddenly, Mark understood. He put an arm around her and pulled her tight, but he was at a loss for comforting words. He knew from experience how empty and trite they could sound.

"There was a big car accident at the hospital today." She seemed to change the subject, but her tone was the same.

"I heard about it," Mark replied. "A van hit a cow, then plowed into another car, right?"

"Yeah, we lost the driver of the other car. Actually, he was DOA, but it's still hard, especially dealing with his family. I don't think I'll ever get used to that."

"I don't think anyone could," Mark replied in a husky tone,

lost in memories of another fatal accident.

"My parents died," Julie broke into his thoughts, "in a car accident. One minute they went to pick up my birthday cake, the next minute they were gone. It still bothers me that I didn't get to say goodbye, you know."

Mark simply nodded, then asked, "How old were you?"

"Eight. At the time, I really didn't understand. I was more upset about missing my birthday party. I'm almost embarrassed to admit that now."

"You were just a kid."

"Reality hit soon enough, though. I had to leave everything behind when I went to New York . . . my friends, my bike, my kittens, my dolls."

"Your dolls?"

"My aunt Stella thought I was too old. Too old for dolls, too old for cartoons, to old to cry if it was thundering outside."

"You can cry now if you want to," he offered gently.

"Thanks, but. . . ." She fought back one sniffle, then another. ". . . But I think the . . . the tears are all . . . dried up . . . by now."

Twenty minutes, and half a box of tissues later, she apologized between residual sniffs, "Sorry about that. I'm just so tired and stressed out today. And I'm sorry I took so long to make my phone call."

"That's all right," Mark assured her, marvelling at how openly she could talk about her past, how freely she could cry for her loved ones, and how quickly she could put it all behind her again. He never talked about the accident that ruined his life, hadn't shed a single tear over it, and it still haunted his every waking hour.

"This night has taught me one thing," Julie remarked forlornly. "I'm not cut out for motherhood."

"Nonsense, with your caring nature, you'll make a wonderful mother someday. The trick is having children one at a time. They're so cute and sweet and helpless as newborns, you're hooked by the time they're old enough to make trouble."

Julie laughed softly, then snuggled up quietly against his shoulder. When she didn't answer his next question, something about if she'd be all right if he headed home, Mark looked down. Julie was sound asleep.

Bless her heart, Mark thought as he pushed an errant lock from her cheek. She was worn out. He knew he really ought to carry her to her bed, but he stroked her soft, dark hair instead.

She looked so peaceful, so beautiful. Her thick lashes lay gracefully against her cheeks. Her lips puckered as she slept, and occasionally she still sniffled. The freckles on her nose begged to be kissed.

Kissed? Oh, what changes Julie had brought to his life. Piece by piece, she was peeling away his armor of numbness. Did he still have a heart under there, or was it too shrivelled from neglect and pain to revive? He'd have to make a commitment to find out. That thought petrified him!

Chapter Twelve

Julie awoke to the mouth-watering smell of bacon. Feeling eight years old again after a night of childhood dreams, it stirred a vision of her mother cooking breakfast while her dad read the paper. Rolling over and stretching, it took a few moments to remember, inch by inch, where she was and why.

Julie flew from the bed. Cody wasn't cooking bacon, was he?! She ran to the kitchen and stopped short. Mark was at the stove, stirring up some scrambled eggs while bacon sizzled on a back burner. Cody sat at the table, and Brandy in her highchair, impatiently awaiting their breakfast.

Spotting Julie in the doorway, Mark smiled at her. "Good morning, sleepyhead! I thought you'd never get up."

"Hi," Julie replied groggily, automatically smoothing her unruly hair. She quickly looked down, a little relieved to see that she had slept in her clothes. Funny, she couldn't even remember getting into bed last night.

"Mornin', Jewsy."

"Ju-Ju!"

"Hi, kids. Did you guys sleep well?"

They both nodded, then clamored for food. Julie helped Mark serve them. As she did, she noticed a dark shadow of whiskers dusting his face. His hair looked uncombed, and he wore the same clothes as last night, though the jacket was missing and his shirt sleeves were rolled up.

Julie was suddenly horrified. "You didn't stay all night here, did you?"

"Hope you don't mind," he replied with a sheepish grin. "My Jeep wouldn't start last night, and it was well after midnight when I tried it. I didn't want to call Steve or Ma to come get me, so I slept on the couch, I promise."

It wasn't that. She didn't think Mark would try anything out of place. But Mrs. Ellsberg wouldn't know that. Julie could just imagine the curtains being pushed aside in the window of the landlady's apartment this morning. *Oh, well!* Julie shrugged. "Do you want me to call a mechanic?"

"It was probably just some moisture on the distributor cap," he replied, shaking his head. "Happens with that old bucket of bolts of mine whenever it rains. It should be dried out by now, though."

"Well, all right then."

The telephone rang, and Julie answered it. "Hello . . . oh, hi. . . . I thought you might . . . at noon . . . all right . . . hey, it's no problem . . . no, we did just fine last night . . . yeah, all right. See you Monday."

When she hung up, she said, "Quit your snickering, Mark. We did do fine last night, thanks to you."

Before Mark could respond, the phone rang again. This time, Julie said, "Hello . . . no, she isn't home . . . oh . . . oh . . . that's too bad. . . . Really? I . . . I probably could do it for you . . . I wouldn't mind at all . . . no problem."

"What was that all about?" Mark asked once the receiver was in its resting place again.

"Well, the first call was Debbie. She and Chip are having such a good time that they decided to stay until Monday. Debbie's mom will come over and pick up the kids about noon."

"And the other call?"

"Oh, that was the Primary president. She was desperate for a substitute for the nursery and hoped that Debbie could do it for her. She's down there all the time with the kids anyway."

"Don't tell me you said that you'd do it?" Mark sounded incredulous.

"Of course," she replied without hesitation. "I can't turn down a chance to serve. Why are you looking at me like that?"

After what he saw last night, Mark was trying to imagine Julie at the mercy of twenty or so toddlers. It wasn't a pretty picture. "You'll have help, won't you?" he asked.

"I don't know. She sounded pretty desperate. But I should be fine. After all, I survived last night, didn't I?"

Mark rolled his eyes. He was becoming an old softie, and he knew it. But concern for the safety of the children of her ward, as well as for Julie's sanity, forced him to say, "Oh, brother. What time do you need me there?"

Mark helped in the nursery the next day as promised. It was a good thing, too, he thought as he wiped twenty-eight pairs of peanut buttery fingerprints off the chairs, the walls, his tie, and Julie's new designer dress of red silk. She didn't seem too upset about the dress, saying her aunt would probably send her another one soon enough.

When the nursery room was finally emptied, Julie coaxed Mark to the chapel for sacrament meeting. He watched her listen to the speakers, wondering how she could look so intent. He'd heard these same boring talks, same long hymns, same old prayers since he was a child. *Same old gossips,* he thought as Mrs. Ellsberg frowned at him and Julie.

After church, Julie invited Mark over for dinner. Despite her lack of culinary skill, she could whip up a mean pot of spaghetti, the one thing she had to show for dating an Italian like Vinny all those years. Mark ate with gusto and complimented her on how good it tasted. She didn't mention it was the only thing she could cook.

When the dishes were done, they decided to go for a ride up through Butterfield Basin. The road was bumpy as they drove through planted fields, then sagebrush-covered terrain. Before long, they were driving along the eastern rim of a deep ravine.

Mark stopped the Jeep, then leaned against it as Julie went over to the edge for a closer look. She could see the river down below, winding between rugged cliffs of sandy brown. A large bird with a white head was drifting through the air . . . below her!

"Look!" Julie called back to Mark. "It's the eagle!"

"Must have a nest around here," he answered from where he stood. "I've seen it a couple of times since that day we met in the corn field."

"Did those poor little plants ever survive my trampling on them?"

"Actually, they're the biggest stalks in the field now. The trauma must have done them good."

"I've heard that real growth comes after a period of adversity," Julie observed. "I've been through a lot of stress and look how strong I am." She flexed her right arm as if to prove her point.

"You call that a muscle?" Mark laughed and held up his own arm. "Now this is a muscle!"

Julie shadow-boxed playfully. "I dare you to come over here and say that, buster."

"No, thanks. In fact, get away from that edge yourself before you fall off or something."

As Julie walked over to him, she teased, "If I didn't know better, I'd say you had a fear of heights."

"Not a fear really," he insisted, holding his arms out to her invitingly. "A dislike of them, maybe, but that's all."

"A big strong guy like you?" she slipped into the warmth of his embrace. It felt good, even if they were just friends. She purred, "These muscles of yours are mighty fine, I must admit."

"Think so?" he asked softly.

"Sure. You must have had a lot of trauma and stress in your life."

"The last few years have been full of it," Mark said in a voice heavy with irony. "But I don't feel any stronger for it."

"You have to be," she insisted, looking up at him intently.

"Otherwise, how did you get to be so thoughtful and kind and wonderful? If you were like this before, I can't understand why Denise ever left you."

Mark didn't answer, but hugged her tight. She felt good in his arms. In fact, he hadn't felt this good in a long, long time. Five years ago—no, longer than that. Had he felt this good ever?

Julie brought out the best in him. He found himself wanting to please her as he never had with Denise. Maybe being alone had helped him appreciate being with someone again. Maybe he had grown a little.

As they gazed at each other, the electricity between them grew. Julie wondered if Mark might kiss her. Mark wondered if anything could stop him from kissing her. They leaned together slowly, naturally. It was a moment of magic, a moment of wonder, a moment of. . . .

"Hey, you two!"

The magical moment was shattered by the crunch of horse's hooves on the graveled road. Mark cursed under his breath while Julie pulled away and ran her fingers quickly through her hair. The intruder was Rick, oblivious to what he was disrupting.

"Man, am I glad to see you, Mark. I tried calling this morning, but you weren't home."

"Believe it or not, I was at church."

"Again? Really?" Rick turned to Julie, as he raised one eyebrow in question.

"Mark came and helped me in the nursery," she explained.

"The nursery?" Rick looked like he wanted to laugh, but he didn't. He didn't want to discourage any contact Mark had with the Church. So he joked, "That couldn't be worse than teaching a bunch of deacons. Hey, I need to ask a favor, old buddy, old pal."

"Shoot," Mark offered, knowing Rick well enough to know that whatever followed was bound to mean trouble.

"The scouts are having a campout this coming week, and I need an extra pair of hands. Brother Foster was supposed to go, but. . . ."

"George Foster?" Julie asked. "I took his x-rays and helped set his leg earlier this week. He's not going to be on his feet for a month, maybe two."

"Exactly," Rick nodded. "So how about it, Mark? We're leaving in the morning, and we'll be back on Friday."

Mark couldn't turn him down. But as he went to the Jeep to get something to write down the directions to the campsite, he grumbled to Julie, "You're having a bad influence on me, woman. Church three weeks in a row, and now a scout camp. Good grief!"

With his back turned to them, Rick winked and gave her the thumbs-up sign. Julie beamed. This was turning out better than she thought. She didn't even mind, too much, that the kiss was abandoned and the magical moment leading up to it never returned. Maybe there was hope for Mark's soul yet.

While the men were gone to scout camp, Rick's wife Annie invited Julie out to the ranch for dinner one night. Julie was more than a little restless, so she readily agreed to come. When she insisted upon bringing something, Annie said a dessert would be good. Julie talked Debbie into making a big batch of cookies.

As she left the apartment to get them, Julie noticed a paper taped to her front door. It was a xeroxed copy of her contract, apparently from Mrs. Ellsberg. The section about no overnight guests was circled in red.

"At least it wasn't the part about no pets allowed," Debbie tried to comfort her fuming friend as she packed warm cookies into a large bowl.

"True," Julie agreed, thinking she would rather be homeless than give up Uncle Sam, even though "he" turned out to be a female kitten. "But still, such a lack of privacy is hard to tolerate. Why can't she just leave me alone?"

"Maybe she's jealous," Debbie noted irreverently as she snapped the lid onto the bowl.

Julie started to giggle and couldn't stop. She and Debbie were soon rolling in laughter. It was some time before Debbie wiped her eyes and said, "Hey, as long as you and Mark know the truth about what happened, or didn't happen, then don't worry about it. Nobody's going to put much stock into what the old snoop has to say anyway."

Julie hoped her friend was right. She wasn't overly concerned for herself. She didn't know most people in town and didn't care what they thought of her. She hated putting any more black marks on Mark's name, though, especially since he hadn't exaggerated their opinions of divorce in the first place.

Julie couldn't shake thoughts of Mark all the way to Birch Creek. She hoped he wasn't too miserable with the scouts. Rick would take good care of him, though. She almost couldn't wait until he returned so she could take over the task herself. After all, what were friends for?

They were still friends, weren't they? Of course they were, no matter what Debbie thought. When she had found out that Mark not only helped with the kids at the apartment, but helped in the nursery the next day as well, she admonished, "You'd better not let him get away, Julie."

"Get away from what? We're just friends!"

"Well, they say that friendship is important in a marriage."

"Who said anything about marriage?"

"Nobody," Debbie had answered simply. "I have a feeling about the two of you."

Julie had no intention of marrying anyone for a good, long time, so she chose to ignore her friend's prediction. She was enjoying her independence too much. Marriage was a fuzzy dream, something to do . . . someday in the future. But for now, she wasn't ready.

If she did ever marry, though, a man like Mark wouldn't be too bad. At least, he wasn't tied to his mother's apron strings like Vinny LaRosa had been. She once blamed their parting of ways on her baptism, but now she realized it was just the last straw in their already-crumbling relationship.

Still, Vinny hadn't been able to accept her membership in the Church. Would Mark be any better? He was a member, but resented the Church all the same. Making a choice between Vinny and the Church had been easy, but with Mark? Nonsense, they were just good friends.

The breeze was cool at the mouth of Snow Canyon as Julie reached the Lees' ranch. She exchanged a nuzzled greeting with Little Al over the fence of a nearby field, then walked over to the house. A host of young faces jostled with each other at the door as they tried to let her in.

"This was so kind of you to invite me," Julie commented as she handed the bowl of cookies to Annie.

"I was purely selfish in doing so," Annie confessed, lifting the plastic cover for a peek at the treats. The children licked their lips with delight when a mouth-watering aroma escaped. "I haven't talked to a grownup in days. I hope you like peas and potatoes. The garden is growing in leaps and bounds this year."

Julie had never tasted fresh, green peas and small, new potatoes, smothered in a rich, creamy sauce. It was delicious, as was the sliced ham, fresh green salad, and homemade rolls that accompanied it. As Julie thought, the cookies were a hit when dinner was over.

The women walked out to the porch and talked as the children, all six of them, scampered around the yard. Annie watched them play. "You know, Rick and Mark swung on that same old tire when they were boys. They delighted in tormenting me from there whenever I came over to play with Rick's little sister."

"You're from Birch Creek, too, then?"

"I am. Born and raised here. Rick and I dated all through high school. In fact, there was only one summer when we tried dating other people. Obviously, it didn't work."

"Was that the summer Mark met Denise at the rodeo?"

"One and the same," she replied, surprised that Mark had told Julie about his failed marriage. It was a taboo topic of discussion for any of the rest of them. "The high and mighty Denise."

"You didn't like her, I take it."

"What was to like?" Annie said in a tone of disgust. "She stole one of our best friends and dragged him off to California. When they finally came back, we tried to be her friend, but she was too good for us."

Secretly pleased, Julie listened with interest as Annie continued, "No one in the ward liked her either. She was either bored or condescending or simply not around . . . never home, you know. Poor Mark put up with a lot. I don't know how he put up with her as long as he did. But listen to me go on. Now tell me, what secret, creative talents do you possess?"

"Not many. Why do you want to know?"

"I'm the homemaking leader in our ward, and I need one more class for next week's meeting."

"Well, I'm afraid I'm not much help then. The only thing my aunt could find for me to do that was even remotely artistic was making pottery."

"Pottery? Like with a wheel and everything?" When Julie nodded, she exclaimed, "Come and give us a demonstration then. We've never had anything like that in Birch Creek before."

"It isn't something that others could participate in," Julie protested, thinking she wasn't good enough to have people watching her.

"It can be a demonstration then, and it only needs to last a half hour or so. Say you'll do it, please!"

Julie agreed, thinking she owed Annie something for the wonderful evening of family fun. As she reluctantly returned to her empty apartment, Julie longed for a family of her own. Maybe having children, one at a time, wouldn't be so bad after all.

Chapter Thirteen

At the end of the week, Julie was at work when the bell over the door jingled. She glanced up to see Mark, looking as good as ever. His hair was still wet, and he smelled of soap and aftershave. His blue eyes twinkled, and his crooked smile was warm.

She sprang from the chair and gave him a hug. Mark chuckled, "Hey, maybe I'll leave more often."

She punched him on the arm. "Don't you dare!"

"You missed me then?"

"I'll never tell," she teased.

It was a slow shift, so she invited him to sit down. As she sorted charting forms, he told her about his camping trip. She laughed heartily as he described some of the scouts' more adventurous escapades.

When he was done, Julie reported her activities. He seemed pleased she had spent time with Annie. But when she told him about the upcoming pottery demonstration, Mark's response surprised her.

"No way!"

"What are you talking about?"

"I'll go to church and listen to you talk. I'll go to scout camp. I'll even help in the nursery," Mark shook his head with determination, "but I draw the line at Relief Society. I'm won't go, so don't even ask!"

"I hadn't thought of it," Julie laughed, "but now that you mention it. . . ."

"No!"

"I could use some help with my potter's wheel."

"No."

"It is so heavy."

"No. . . ."

"And with muscles like those. . . ."

"Oh, you could sweet talk a grizzly bear," Mark groaned. "I'll carry in your darned wheel, but that's it. Hey, you working tomorrow?"

"No, why?"

"Wanna put your muscles to the test? We're hauling hay again, and we're short a couple of hands."

"Sounds like fun."

"Fun?" he replied doubtfully. "It's darn hard work."

"I'll eat my Wheaties then," she promised.

After making arrangements for the morning, he said goodbye. As he left, a young mother came in with a crying baby. When he got to the Jeep, he remembered that he had left his keys on Julie's desk. As he walked back in the hospital, Julie was blowing up a rubber glove like a balloon. The fingers stuck out from the rounded hand like fat porcupine quills.

Knowing Julie, he thought, she probably would find something fun about hauling hay. Actually, the possibility of having her there made it sound more fun for him as well. Would she even be able to budge a bale of hay, though? She was such a scrawny thing—although just in the right places.

The following morning, Julie met Mark at the old West farm. Gus was moving soon and couldn't be bothered to harvest what few crops he had gotten around to planting in the spring. Hating to see it go to waste, the Jacksons were hustling to bring in the hay before it was too late.

Dressed in an old New York Knicks T-shirt and ragged jeans, Julie sat beside Mark on the back of an empty trailer which was being pulled by a large, green tractor. As it bounced over the ruts,

Mark put an arm around Julie's shoulder to keep her from falling, he claimed. It didn't stop his nephews from teasing him, however, and Mark formulated plans to get even with them later.

They crossed a canal, then stopped in a field where square bales of hay dotted the stubbly ground at random. They split into teams, some throwing hay onto the trailer while others stacked it. Julie put on her gloves, ready to pitch right in.

Mark made the work look easy, swinging the large bales with ease. Julie reached for one, stalling under the weight of it. She strained and worked, worked and strained to get it to budge an inch. Exhausted, she paused for a quick breather.

Mark walked over to her. "No slacking allowed, woman."

"I probably should have had a few more traumatic experiences in my life, because my muscles aren't quite up to this challenge."

"Or maybe a few more Wheaties. Why don't you ride awhile?"

He helped her up onto the highest level of stacked bales. Despite the prickly hay she could feel through her jeans, she felt like a queen, watching the activity below her from an unlikely throne. *What a scruffy-looking kingdom,* she thought with a smile.

When the trailer wouldn't hold another bale, they returned to the West farm, working in reverse to stack the hay in a barn there. They repeated the entire process two more times. Julie tried to do her part, glad as anyone when it was time to stop for lunch.

Sarah, Joyce, and little Thad brought them sandwiches and lemonade. Mark chose a quiet spot in the shade by the old farmhouse to eat, and Julie joined him. They ate in silence for a few minutes, Mark scowling as he studied his surroundings.

Finally, he spoke wistfully, "This land has been in the family ever since the first West family came to Birch Creek as pioneers."

"It would be a shame to see it go into a stranger's hands then," Julie expressed Mark's exact sentiments about the impending sale. "Any interested buyers?"

"Sam Watkins would love to get his hands on it," Mark replied bitterly. "I'd hate to see that happen. I swear he's determined to own all of Birch Creek someday."

"Isn't there anything you can do to stop him?" Julie wanted to know.

"I don't know of anything, short of buying the farm myself."

They both paused a minute as the idea took hold. Julie looked around with an appraising gaze. Mark opened his mouth to speak, then closed it again as he seriously considered doing such a thing. They looked at each other and grinned.

She was the first to talk. "You should own this land you love so much. You could fix up the house. . . ."

". . . And paint the barn. . . ."

". . . And trim the fruit trees. . . ."

". . . And weed the gardens. . . ."

". . . And get your own horses."

"I like the way you think, woman," he grinned. "You know, I'm going to seriously check into this whole thing. Why didn't I think of it before?"

During the next week, Oakwood prepared for its big summer celebration—Pioneer Days, held on the 24th of July. The whole town went overboard to honor its heritage. Covered wagons and western wear prevailed.

When the big day arrived, Mark and Julie spent it together. They went to a chuckwagon breakfast at sunrise. They visited the pioneer museum and browsed at the sidewalk sale. They sat with Debbie and Chip during the parade.

After the parade was over, Mark and Julie wandered over to the city's baseball field where the carnival was in full swing. Mark won a stuffed bear for Julie on the midway. They rode a few rides, but Mark refused to go on the rickety ferris wheel.

"Not afraid of heights, huh?" she teased. "You'd never make it in a high-rise apartment building."

His reply had a double meaning. "I certainly hope I never have to try."

All day long, they had been munching on everything in sight. Julie was surprised that she didn't get a bellyache. Mark wasn't so lucky. They had just enough time to get a little antacid for him before the rodeo started.

The events of the rodeo passed quickly . . . calf roping, steer wrestling, barrel racing, bareback riding. A peppery commentator made jokes over the loudspeaker. A live country band played background music from the broadcast booth.

The final event of the evening, bull-riding, was definitely the most exciting. Julie marvelled at the sheer size of the animals, the strength of the cowboys who rode them, and the reckless courage of the clowns who flirted with danger by distracting them away from the downed riders. Julie was glad for the wooden fence that separated the huge bulls from the spectators.

Although the final ride of the night was now history, the clowns still wanted to play with the last bull, a massive beast with long horns. They teased it, one dashing back and forth while another hid in the barrel. The bull pawed the ground and charged. The crowd gasped and cheered.

Tired of the game, the bull searched out the gate to the corral. It lunged and missed, breaking through the very fence Julie had just been appreciating. Landing with a thud on the boardwalk, the bull missed the legs of some very stunned rodeo-goers by inches.

Screaming, people scattered as fast as they could go. The bull, unable to find its footing on the plank floor, bellowed with rage. Quick action by the men at the gate had the fence dismantled, freeing the enraged animal.

Julie and Mark escaped unscathed, strolling slowly through the quiet of a baseball diamond just beyond the carnival lights. Suddenly someone came running towards them. It was Woody. He was out of breath and talking so fast that neither of them could understand a word he was saying.

"Slow down, buddy," Mark put a firm hand on the young Indian's shoulder. "Now what's this about Troy?"

"He's really sick," Woody managed between panting breaths. "He can't hardly breathe."

"Where is he?" The concern was evident in Julie's voice.

Woody led them to a darkened dugout nearby. Gary was there, pacing nervously. They didn't see Troy at first, but they could hear his groaning. As their eyes adjusted to the darkness, they saw him lying prone on the bench.

Julie was at his side instantly, assessing him as best she could. While she did, Mark questioned both Woody and Gary about what had happened. Neither of them said much, humming and hawing and kicking at the ground.

"His heart is beating a hundred miles an hour," Julie said quickly when she was done. "He's trembling, and even in here, I can tell he's white as a ghost. He says his head aches and his mouth is dry."

"What does that mean?"

"It means he needs medical attention. We'd better get him over to the hospital."

Gary's car was nearby. To everyone's surprise, Troy jumped off the bench and fought off the hands offered him when it was time to go. He made it to the car without falling, and the rest of them piled in around him for the short ride to the hospital.

When they reached the emergency entrance, Troy was too dizzy to walk at all. Mark and Woody supported him under the arms, easing him onto a stretcher inside. The nurse on duty moaned when she saw them.

Two of her stretchers were already filled by people from the rodeo. The bull had landed on the foot of one, and another was having heart palpitations from fright. Julie offered to take over Troy's care for now, and the nurse readily agreed to let her.

Julie told Gary and Woody to wait outside, but allowed Mark to stay as she drew the striped curtains around them. Troy immediately sat up and made good on a declaration that he was going to be sick. She wiped his mouth with a tissue, then put a cold cloth on his forehead.

Troy couldn't seem to settle down. With one hand held to his chest, and the other to his head, he whimpered like a child one minute, then kicked and fought the next. Between outbursts, Julie hooked him up to a heart monitor, took his vital signs, and started an I.V.

She didn't dare medicate him, though, until she knew what was wrong. And to figure that out, she needed answers to some questions. Troy was resting momentarily, so she pulled Mark outside the curtain where she could still watch her patient.

"How is he?" Mark asked with quiet concern.

"He's stable, but his heart is racing at a dangerous rate."

"Why is that?"

"I don't know for sure," Julie was reluctant tell Mark her suspicions. "But it looks like some kind of a drug overdose."

"Drugs?" Mark spat out the word. "If I find out that those boys have been getting messed up in that stuff. . . ."

Julie grabbed his arm to stop him from stomping out of the room. "If it was drugs, find out what kind it was, how much he took, and when, okay?"

Mark nodded and was off in search of Gary and Woody. Judging by the look on his face, Julie was glad that she wasn't in their shoes about now. Troy seemed stable, but Julie hovered over him anyway, doing what she could to make him comfort. She wished that Mark would hurry.

When he did return, he pulled a plastic bag out of his pocket and threw it to her. A few pills remained in the bottom. "There's the culprit. They weren't sure how many he took, but it was sometime between eight and nine."

Julie took out one of the small, white pills and studied it with a frown. It looked vaguely familiar. She noted the number code imprinted on one side and the manufacturer's symbol on the other. Hmm . . . she pulled out a large drug reference book and opened to the gray pages where the pictures of different pills were. Julie checked each picture carefully and finally found what she was looking for. She shook her head sadly.

Mark, who had been watching carefully, whispered, "Bad?"

"Not really bad," Julie replied, "but kind of sad. How much

did Troy pay for this little bag of pills?"

"Fifty dollars or so. Why?"

"It's pseudoephedrine."

"What's that?" Mark questioned.

"Just a decongestant, a cold pill. You can get them at any pharmacy for under five dollars."

"Somebody sold him a bag of cold pills, telling him he'd get a real buzz off them? I can't believe it. And why would he try them in the first place?"

Julie didn't have an answer. Dr. Poplin appeared, barking orders for her to carry out as soon as he had examined Troy. He didn't seem to notice that Julie wasn't officially on duty. She jumped to comply, deferring only one task to the regular nurse.

As she approached Troy with a urinary catheter to monitor his output, the teenager sat up and bellowed, "You're putting what where?"

With a smile, Julie began the paperwork to admit Troy as the doctor had ordered. Mark went off to send the other boys home. To save Julie the anguish of dealing with family, Mark offered to call his brother with the news. He dreaded the task, putting it off as long as he dared.

Steve and Joyce would be upset, to say the least. They tried hard to raise their boys properly, and Troy was a pretty good kid. Maybe a little rebellious lately, but he was a teenager, wasn't he? With a heavy heart, Mark made the call.

Then he went to the room where Troy had been taken in his absence. Once he arrived, Julie left with a handful of papers. Mark pulled a chair up to the head of Troy's bed. The boy's eyes flickered open.

"You're not going to tell Mom and Dad, are you?" he asked in a groggy whisper.

Mark didn't tell him that the deed was already done. Instead, he asked, "And how else do you plan on explaining where you've been all night?"

"I could say I slept over at Gary's, or Woody's. Mom doesn't know his family at all."

"And how do you plan on explaining the hospital bill?"

Troy opened his mouth, but then closed it without a word. There was no explaining it. He was in trouble. And he didn't even get a decent buzz from it. All he got was sick, sick, sick. He looked irritably at Mark.

"Who are you to be lecturing me anyway? I thought if anyone could keep a secret, you could."

"Maybe so, if the secret isn't something that puts you in the hospital. But this is too big—too serious. Why did you do it anyway?"

"Just for fun."

"Fun? Was it fun to have your stomach pumped?"

"Not really, but I didn't think about that. . . ."

"You just didn't think, period."

"One time wasn't going to hurt anything," Troy insisted.

"But it isn't just a one-time thing, Troy. What if there's permanent damage to your heart? What if you can't run track next year? What if you can't do your part on the farm?"

"No great loss," Troy mumbled.

"You'd think so if your father lost everything. He has enough to worry about without worrying about that."

"Serves him right," Troy whined. "He's always nagging at me."

"Maybe because he cares about you. You're supposed to be ordained a priest next week, but Steve tells me you haven't been to church for weeks."

"Hey, you're a great one to talk. You haven't been in years, and you've gotten along just fine."

Mark didn't know what to say. Troy had a good point.

Julie returned, followed shortly thereafter by Steve and Joyce, every bit as upset as Mark imagined. They discussed the situation in the hall, then Troy's parents went inside. With nothing left to do there, Mark and Julie slipped out of the hospital.

The night was clear and cool. Mark tried, but couldn't thank Julie enough for her help. He knew she wouldn't be paid for the long hours she'd spent with Troy.

Julie sensed his feelings. "Don't worry about it! It's just part of the job for a nurse. I can't stop caring when I'm not punching a time clock."

Mark hugged her tightly. "Thanks again. You really are incredible."

As Mark drove home later that night, he felt some hard pains in his stomach. He never realized his own inactivity in the Church was affecting anyone but him. He did what he did for reasons that were his alone. Now to find out he was ultimately responsible for something like this?! He was going to have to be careful, just like in that little poem that kept running through his head.

You must be true in all you do,
Watchful eyes are all about.
You never know what seeds you sow,
Or when those seeds will sprout.

Chapter Fourteen

Mark didn't feel very well for the rest of the weekend, though after the ordeal with Troy, he hated to complain. Even so, he skipped out early from a family reunion on Sunday afternoon. Knowing his dislike for family gatherings, no one thought that too unusual.

On Monday, he didn't feel up to doing chores. But with Troy out of commission, Steve needed the help. So Mark took some antacid and went to work. He went to bed early, though, sleeping well past the morning milking on Tuesday.

In fact, he didn't wake up until Julie called to remind him of her pottery demonstration that night. As he had promised, Mark hauled her potter's wheel from her apartment to the Jeep, from the Jeep to the church in Birch Creek, from the church to the Jeep, then from the Jeep back into her apartment. He left weak and lightheaded by the time he was finished.

Without a word about his infirmity, he excused himself and drove home. Julie was too hyped about how the evening went to notice that anything was wrong with Mark. Her demonstration was over, and she had even made her first official craft, painted blocks of wood glued together to form a little recipe box.

To fill that box, LuAnn Frost presented 101 recipes for fresh zucchini. Through it all, she glared at Julie as if to challenge her to a cooking duel. Julie knew she'd be no match for anyone in the kitchen.

When Annie said LuAnn had had a crush on Mark since grade

school, Julie was surprised to think that she actually felt a strange twinge. Jealous of LuAnn? Ridiculous! Because LuAnn hardly deserved her concern, or because she and Mark were merely friends, Julie wasn't sure.

After Mark left, Julie dressed in a pink nightshirt and went to bed. She couldn't go to sleep right away, so she pulled out her scriptures. It was almost midnight before she drifted off to sleep. Sometime later the telephone jarred Julie from her dreams. Disoriented, she reached over and answered it.

"Julie?"

"Mark?"

"Sorry to wake you, Julie, but my stomach really hurts. I took some more antacid, but it didn't help. Any ideas?"

"Stomach hurts," Julie muttered in a sleepy voice. "It could be gas, especially if it moves around. If it's in one place, it could be something . . . like a kidney . . . stone . . . or maybe . . . a. . . ."

Her words faded away to nothing. After a moment or two of silence, Mark hung up. She must have fallen back to sleep. He wouldn't have called her at all, but he wasn't sure how much more of this pain he could take.

Doubled over, he slowly made his way back to bed. He couldn't sleep, he couldn't rest, and he couldn't keep still. He tried not to look at the clock. That just made things worse. The night was endless as it was.

Julie awoke a few moments later to the loud beeping of a telephone off the hook. The call must have been real. She thought it was a dream. Shaking off cobwebs of sleep as she sat up in bed, she tried to recall the conversation.

She vaguely remembered Mark saying something about his stomach hurting. She pushed Uncle Sam aside, threw off the covers and sprang from her bed. Did she say something about gas? What kind of a dimwitted nurse was she, she wondered as she frantically dialed his number.

While she waited for an answer, she told herself to assess the situation. How long had Mark been sick? He seemed fine tonight, or did he? He, who threw bales of hay around with ease, had huffed and puffed as he carried the potter's wheel.

And didn't his arm feel warm when she thanked him for his help? Well, really, hadn't he been a little under the weather since the carnival? She'd worked some extra shifts, so she wasn't around him a lot to notice. *Oh, please answer!* she cried inwardly.

At last, she heard someone fumble on the other end of the line, then mutter a husky, pain-filled, "Hello?"

"Oh, Mark," Julie rushed with relief. "Sorry, but I was incoherent a few minutes ago. How are you?"

His words sounded strained, "It hurts . . . a lot."

"Where?"

"In . . . my . . . stomach."

"Around your side and into your back?"

"Not really more like low . . . in the front."

"Low in the front. Hmm," she thought a minute. "More on the left or the right?"

"Maybe a little more . . . on the right."

"Do you have a fever?"

"I don't know. I feel . . . pretty cold . . . right now."

"Shivering?"

"Yeah. . . . I can't . . . stop."

Julie frowned. She knew he was no complainer, not after treating that second-degree burn like it was nothing. He must really be in a lot of pain now. It was hard to diagnose over the phone, but she had some suspicions.

"It could be a really bad case of flu," she said at last, "or it could be your appendix. Either way, you'd better get checked. Have Sarah or Steve drive you to the hospital, and I'll meet you there."

"Now? Okay," he mumbled.

As soon as Mark hung up, Julie grabbed a pair of old, gray sweats and threw them on right over her pink nightshirt. The tail of it hung out the back, but Julie didn't notice or care. She grabbed her purse and ran out to the Explorer, finger-combing her hair as she went.

Julie quickly arrived at the Oakwood Hospital. Mark wasn't there yet, so she quickly explained the situation to the nurse on duty. As they worked to get things ready, Julie kept glancing at the entrance. Where was Mark? Maybe she should have gone out and got him herself.

Just when she was ready to drop everything and drive out to Mark's place, headlights lit up the driveway outside. Sarah jumped out of her car, still dressed in her flannel robe and slippers, and Julie rushed out to help her put Mark into a wheelchair. It wasn't an easy task. He moaned when he moved and groaned when he didn't.

He was burning hot, sweating profusely, and very pale. He held one hand to a spot halfway between his belly-button and his right hip bone as Julie pushed the wheelchair inside. With difficulty, he struggled up onto a stretcher.

Julie and the other nurse worked together to take his vital signs, start an I.V., fill out the history forms, and make him as comfortable as possible. They couldn't give him pain medication, however, and that tore at Sarah's heart. She grasped his hand and whispered her concerns to Julie.

"I know what you mean," Julie agreed, not liking to see Mark suffer any more than his mother did, "but the doctor needs to check him first. We can't mask his symptoms."

"Well, I hope he hurries. I found Mark out on the lawn. I don't know how long he was out there. If Max hadn't howled and woke me up, he'd probably still be out there now."

"Good old Max," Julie replied, holding Mark's free arm while her co-worker drew blood for labwork. "He deserves an extra bone today."

"And I'll see that he gets it, too," Sarah assured her.

At last, Dr. Bolinsky arrived. He assured the nurse on duty that he didn't mind being called in, even if it wasn't his turn. Julie had taken a chance by defying the most holy of on-call lists. But she didn't want to trust Mark's care to anyone else.

Thumping on Mark's tender abdomen, Dr. Bolinsky asked, "When did this pain start?"

"The night of the carnival, really. But it didn't get this bad until tonight." Mark spoke through his clenched teeth.

"Temperature?"

"101.8," Julie replied.

"White blood count?"

The other nurse supplied that information, "16.3. Everything else was within normal ranges."

Dr. Bolinsky finished his examination and looked at Mark. "I believe your appendix is hot, old boy, and there's only one cure for that: get rid of it. It's almost five now, and anesthesia will be coming from Logan about seven anyway. I'll bump my other cases back and do you first before the darn thing ruptures."

Mark readily agreed, especially when the doctor ordered a pain shot while they waited. Julie quickly had him sign the necessary consents for surgery while the other nurse drew up the medication. Sarah left to call home.

A few minutes later, Steve bustled in. He'd slipped down quickly before morning chores, but he couldn't stay. The cows could wait, though, until he gave his brother a blessing. Dr. Bolinsky offered to assist.

Julie felt touched as the priesthood holders put their hands upon Mark's head and blessed him with strength to endure the surgery. Near the end of the blessing, Steve said, "Mark, you'll recover fully. Something special waits for you, and you'll be able to fulfill that mission."

Then Mark was whisked off to the operating room. Julie waited with Sarah in the lobby. Neither spoke much, but both fidgeted. Sarah thought of the simple surgery that had taken her husband's life. Julie thought of the countless complications that could arise. Both thought of the words of the blessing. Mark would fully recover.

It seemed like forever before Dr. Bolinsky came out in his

green scrubs and told them that everything went well. The appendix hadn't ruptured yet, but it fell apart in his hands as he removed it. Mark was in the recovery room now, but was still heavily sedated.

As Sarah called the family again, Julie wandered down to the recovery room where Mark rested on a stretcher. Julie bent down to kiss him, despite an oxygen mask covering the lower half of his face. She pushed it aside a moment.

Something wasn't right. His breathing seemed awfully slow and shallow. Sometimes, he hardly breathed at all. She glanced up at the vital sign monitor. His blood pressure, 82/48, flashed off and on in red. The alarm's volume had been turned down to almost nothing.

Julie tried to arouse Mark. He moaned briefly, and one eye fluttered open. His pupil was the size of a pinpoint. That wasn't good. Julie pushed the button on the machine again: 78/44.

"Hey," Julie called to the recovery room nurse, "we've got a problem over here!"

"Oh, dear," the nurse threw Mark's chart aside. "Is that blood pressure right?"

"Afraid so," Julie replied as she tried to arouse Mark again. He had almost no response at all. In a matter of seconds, his pressure dropped from 72/40 to 52/34. His abdomen was flat, his dressing dry, no bleeding. What could it be?

Increasing his I.V. rate, Julie asked, "Has he been medicated?"

"I gave him twenty-five of Demerol I.V. about ten minutes ago. He seemed stable enough. Maybe it was too much too soon."

Together, they lifted the foot of his stretcher. Even so, his blood pressure read 44/25. People didn't live with pressures that low. Mark was quickly slipping into a painless and eternal sleep. They had to act quickly, before it was too late!

"Do you have some Narcan?" Julie asked, telling herself not to panic.

"Right here," the nurse responded as she fumbled to break the top of the glass ampule of narcotic antagonist. "Half of this to begin with, right?"

Julie's mind travelled a million miles an hour, trying to remember. She couldn't let anything happen to Mark! "Yeah, yeah, and if it doesn't work, then give the other half. Hurry!"

As the medication was given, Julie paged Dr. Bolinsky. He arrived just moments later. He quickly checked Mark. "Good work, ladies. And nice uniform, Julie. Those sweats and that pink nightshirt really brighten up this place."

Julie didn't mind his comment, for Mark was improving rapidly. His blood pressure was 86/52 and climbing. His pulse was strong, and his pupils looked normal. He was muttering something under his breath; Julie hoped it was about pain. At this point, pain was good, pain would keep him awake, pain meant life!

As she gazed down upon him, Julie was overcome with a wonderfully frightening feeling. It made her heart swell and brought tears to her eye. It made her want to sing, turn cartwheels, and thank the Lord, all at the same time. It made what she had felt for Vinny LaRosa seem like a silly crush.

These were no feelings of friendship, nor was it a crush. She loved Mark! Loved him with the kind of love that Brother and Sister Montague shared, the kind of love that she imagined her parents shared, the kind of love that could last a lifetime.

"Oh, Mark." She bent over, brushing sandy hair off his forehead before placing a kiss upon his whisker-roughened cheek. Still he repeated the same thing over and over. It sounded like "lady." Was he talking to the recovery room nurse?

The more alert Mark became, the clearer his words were. It wasn't lady he was saying. It was "Sadie." Who was Sadie? And why was Mark saying how sorry he was to leave her? Wasn't his first wife named Denise? Julie was sure of it.

Good grief! She had just realized her love for Mark, and already she had unknown competition. LuAnn Frost, she could handle, but who was this Sadie? Why would Mark utter her name on the brink of death? He was stable now, so she left him in the care of the recovery room nurse, told his mother that all was well, and went home to change.

Even as she sat at his bedside later, she couldn't shake the gloomy feeling settling over her. Mark's blood pressure was 118/64, and his temperature a mere 100.4 degrees. He was still groggy, though. And every once in awhile, as he slept, Julie thought she heard the name Sadie.

Exhausted physically and emotionally, she finally decided to go back home and get some sleep. As she stood up, Mark stirred and reached a hand to her. "Going already?"

"Yeah," she took his hand. "I've got to work tomorrow, and I've got to feed the cat. But you're in good hands here."

He squeezed her hand tightly and replied, "These are the best hands, though. Thanks for being there for me. Hey, Julie?"

"Yes?"

Dr. Bolinsky came in right then, interrupting the moment. By the time he left, Mark was asleep. Julie went home, puzzled. *Was he about to confess something about the mysterious Sadie? Was he going to thank her again? Or did he just need a drink of water?*

Julie stopped by Mark's room on her way to work the following morning. She was tickled to see him wide awake, sitting up in bed, and begging for breakfast. He didn't remember a thing about the previous day, however. Everything between carrying her potter's wheel and talking to her now was a blank.

Over the next few days, Julie filled him in on the details. Mark was feeling good, but his temperature wouldn't come down enough to go home. So he wandered around the hospital, pushing his I.V. for antibiotics on a pole beside him. He was a frequent visitor of the emergency room when Julie was there.

They talked and laughed, but mostly, he watched her work. She handled each situation, from crisis to crybabies, with ease. Was this the same Julie who cried on her first day of driving lessons and jumped at the crack of thunder?

Had others seen her more vulnerable side? With a strong wave of possessiveness, he hoped not. He wanted to be the only one who could comfort her. Why? She was a good friend and all, but he wasn't ready for more. Maybe it was the drugs. Maybe they were clouding his thinking. He'd act like everything was normal until his head cleared, and then he could figure it out.

Unmindful of his thoughts, it was equally hard for Julie to act like Mark was just a friend, instead of the object of her love. He didn't mention Sadie again, and the time never seemed right for her to ask. Until that issue was resolved, Julie put her feelings aside. Having him on the road to recovery was enough.

By Sunday morning, Mark's temperature reached an acceptable 98.8 degrees, so Dr. Bolinsky discharged him with instructions to take it easy for a week or two. Julie was there and promised that Mark would comply—even if she had to tie him to his couch and take away the keys to his tractor.

Once Julie got him home, she fussed over him all afternoon. She made a bed for him on his sofa when he refused to go to bed. She brought him lunch from Sarah's and made sure he took his pills. She answered his every need, often before he even expressed them.

She made sure that all of Mark's well-wishers didn't stay long. Most went willingly although it was hard to convince Thad that Mark needed his rest. And LuAnn Frost, who arrived with a pot of soup, wouldn't be convinced at all. She wanted the role of Mark's caregiver for herself, so she stayed . . . and stayed.

It wasn't jealousy, Julie insisted, that motivated her to forget tact and literally boot the intruder out the door. Well, maybe it was jealousy, Julie conceded as she fed LuAnn's soup to old Max. They ate canned soup for their dinner, but Mark didn't seem to mind.

Afterwards, they sat on the sofa and talked. Both sensed that their relationship had moved into a deeper realm since his surgery, but neither wanted to discuss it. Instead, Julie told him of the healing blessing.

At the mention of a mission, Mark snorted, "I'm not going on a mission, and that's that!"

"You don't necessarily have to go on a mission," Julie explained, "to fulfill the mission of your life. Coming to Oakwood was a mission of sorts for me. I felt like the Lord needed me here. I still don't know why, but I'll figure it out."

"Maybe you were supposed to save my life," he suggested flippantly. Then he remembered how she broke through his cocoon of numbness to strip away his loneliness. "In more ways than one," he added quietly.

With a smile, she replied, "Maybe so."

Chapter Fifteen

Julie made sure Mark followed the doctor's instructions to take it easy to the letter. He was not allowed to do any work on the farm. While Mark had been hospitalized, July had turned into August and there was much to be done. But Julie was firm. He wasn't going anywhere.

Mark wandered around the house until he thought he would go nuts. He wandered over to Sarah's and watched her do her canning. He wandered around the yard and watched the boys doing their chores—actually they were his chores, but the boys didn't mind taking over. Even Troy, who was stronger now, didn't complain too much.

If Mark ever wandered down to the milking barn, Steve had strict instructions to send him back to the house. His follow-up appointment with Dr. Bolinsky wasn't until Friday, and he wasn't even allowed to drive until then. Without a doubt, Mark was going stir-crazy.

Thursday was Julie's day off, so she drove up to the farm and took Mark for a ride. He was glad for the escape. For a recovering workaholic, a week of leisure was a hard sentence.

They drove past the old West farm where a group of people were packing the Gledhill's things into a large moving van. Mark and Julie decided to watch from the shade of a large weeping willow tree on the lawn of the church. They laughed at the fact that most men could carry out two or three boxes to Gus' one.

As they watched, Mark said, "I approached Ma with the idea

of buying the farm the other day."

"What did she say?" Julie asked excitedly.

"She liked it. I don't think she really wanted to sell the land, but she just got tired of worrying about it. She quoted me a price, and it's a steal. I tried to argue, but she said it was non-negotiable. I've got an appointment next week with Mr. Standish at the bank to talk about a loan."

"Great! What will you do with the farmhouse? Rent it?"

"Well," he paused and looked at her sideways. "I'm thinking of moving in myself. I'd kind of like to fix things up in memory of Grandpa and Grandma. They took such pride in their home."

Resting a hand gently on his arm, she replied, "I think that's neat. Beneath your gruff exterior lies a heart of gold, mister."

"Yeah, right."

As Mark told her his plans for the farm, his excitement was contagious, and before long, she was curious to see what the large farmhouse looked like on the inside. Was it rundown? Was it salvageable? Was it a home that could be filled with love? Julie mentally began creating a warm, cozy picture.

Humph! Julie shook the picture from her mind. Mark's moving in didn't have anything to do with her. Never once had he suggested anything more than friendship between them. Any thoughts of a future with him were in her own imagination.

And speaking of imagination, who was this mysterious Sadie? Was she a childhood sweetheart Mark had never forgotten? Or a current love Julie didn't know about? Was Sadie the reason Mark insisted they were only friends? Or had Julie imagined that whole thing, too?

Julie had to know. Mark looked fairly relaxed now, leaning back on one elbow like that. He was quiet, lost in thoughts—she hoped—about the old farm he loved so much. It was now or never.

"Mark, can I ask you something?" she said softly to break the silence that had fallen over them. "Something personal?"

"Shoot." He squinted up at her. The sunlight created a golden halo around her dark hair. Pretty. He wanted to grant her the world and then some.

With a deep breath, she asked, “Who is Sadie?”

She could feel the air immediately bristle with tension. Mark didn’t answer, but just looked off into the distance with a scowl. Waiting patiently for his answer, Julie hoped she hadn’t made a mistake by asking.

When he finally spoke, his tone was menacing. “Who told you about Sadie?”

“You did.”

“Me?”

“When you were waking up from the anesthesia after your surgery,” Julie explained, “you mentioned her name over and over.”

“I did?” Mark couldn’t remember that. He couldn’t remember anything about the surgery or the anesthesia or Sadie. At last, he struggled to his feet, sighing, “It’s probably as easy to show you as tell you about her.”

Very puzzled now, Julie took his offered hand. He didn’t say another word, but slowly led her up the quiet lane to the cemetery beyond the church. Julie hoped the walk wasn’t too much for Mark. Considering their destination, however, she guessed that his pained expression came from the heart.

Once inside the graveyard, Julie stepped carefully to avoid thistles that dotted the grass. It wasn’t easy to keep up with Mark’s determined stride. At last, he stopped near a small, gray headstone within the West family plot. Julie knelt down for a closer look.

Brushing off dried grass clippings, she saw tiny hearts and lambs and fat cherubs engraved on the headstone. A child was buried there. The dates she uncovered revealed it was barely two years old when it died. The name . . . SADIE LEE JACKSON.

“Oh.” Julie couldn’t think of anything else to say as she ran a finger gently over the cold stone. Was Sadie Mark’s sister? Or a niece? Then an even sadder thought struck Julie. She looked up into Mark's troubled eyes, and he nodded.

Julie felt her heart contract within her chest. Sadie was Mark's child. From the dates on the headstone, Mark and Denise's child. Julie wanted to know more, but was afraid to ask.

Mark sank down heavily beside her. He struggled to find words to explain, but how could he talk about something he had refused to think about for five years? After several long moments, he found his voice, raspy and low.

"She was the reason Denise and I stayed together as long as we did. Remember how Denise wanted to stay in L.A. when I finished school? Well, after I accepted the job in Idaho, she found out she was pregnant. I think she disliked the thought of going through that alone worse than she disliked the thought of living in Birch Creek. So in the end, she came back with me.

"I was glad because that saved me a fight for custody after the baby was born. There was no way I was going to let a child of mine be raised in that city. We came back in June, and she was born the following February."

He paused momentarily, and Julie placed a reassuring hand upon his shoulder. Giving it a squeeze, he went on, "Denise and I still didn't get along very well. We tried at first . . . for the baby's sake. But even that didn't help for long. We just had different ideas of what was worthwhile. Denise wasn't about to let a child cramp her style, so I tended her a lot while her mother was off with friends in Logan."

No wonder Mark is so good with kids, Julie thought. No wonder he could handle Cody and Brandy the night of the storm and was always so cute with Thad. He'd had a lot of practice . . . with his own child. Julie was touched. When Mark paused again, she asked, "What happened?"

As if his strength gave out, Mark fell back onto the grass. Staring up at the sky, he said, "When she was just two, Denise and I had a big fight. She wanted to go out. I thought I could use a little time to myself to grade school papers. I told Denise she wasn't much of a mother, leaving her child behind all the time.

Out to prove me wrong, she bundled up the baby and took off. I'm not sure where they were headed."

Mark paused and took a deep breath. Julie moved closer, and Mark rested his head in her lap. She softly stroked his hair as he continued in a quiet voice, "They didn't get very far from the farm, just a couple of miles really, when the accident happened."

"Accident?" Julie's heart skipped a beat.

"Yeah. Remember Sam Watkins? Well, his brother Clem used to go to town every Saturday night and make the rounds of all the bars before he came home. He'd had a few too many, as usual, and plowed right into them. Denise never made the baby keep her seat belt on, and she was killed instantly. Thank goodness for that, anyway."

Mark's voice broke at that point, and Julie sniffled herself as she asked, "And Denise?"

"Had a bunch of bumps and cuts all over, that's all. Old Clem broke his leg."

"That hardly seems fair!" Julie now understood Mark's strong opinions against drinking. She looked over and saw him fighting to keep his emotions at bay. She said gently, "It's okay to cry, even now."

His eyes remained dry as he continued, "I never could cry. I had to be strong. I had to make the funeral and burial arrangements. I had to call the relatives. I had to pack up all her things and carry them to Ma's basement. It's just a blur now. When I think back on it, it seemed like it was always dark . . . a sad, dark time."

"I'll bet it was," Julie spoke with feeling. "Didn't Denise help?"

"She was a basket case. They had to keep her on tranquilizers until the funeral. Even then, she went berserk. Once we were back home, she'd never talk about the baby. Maybe she felt guilty. I know how that hurts. I kept telling myself, if only I hadn't gotten mad at Denise. If only I had kept the baby home. If only, if only. . . ."

His voice trailed off again as long-forgotten regrets surfaced once again. Julie wasn't sure how to help, but she thought talking about it was good. So she asked, "And Denise left not long after that?"

"Yeah, about a month after the accident. She was there one day and gone the next."

"Talk about adding insult to injury," Julie muttered, wondering how Mark's ex-wife could be so heartless.

"I felt abandoned on just about every side," Mark continued. "My baby was gone, my wife was gone, my family couldn't talk about it without crying, and no one in the ward talked about it either. They just pretended like Denise or the baby never existed."

"Maybe they didn't know what to say."

"Maybe, but anything would have been better than nothing, or talking behind your back. I tried to go to church anyway, thinking I'd better shape up if I was ever going to see my little girl again."

"And then?"

"Well, the last straw was when Clem came back to church a month or so later, using a cane and all. Everyone rushed up to greet him, gushing about how sorry they were about the accident. How was his leg? How was his car? How was his farm? And not one word to me. I couldn't handle it. I didn't need a church where people acted like that."

"You can't judge the whole Church by the actions of a few."

"Yeah, well, I guess I wasn't in a real philosophical mood at the time," Mark snapped. After a poignant pause, he said, "Sorry about that. It wasn't your fault."

"That's all right," Julie shrugged. He wasn't really lashing out at her, and she knew it. "I'm just wondering why Clem was at church? I mean, didn't he serve time in jail?"

"Naw," Mark spoke with bitterness as he pulled away from Julie. "They just slapped him on the wrist. After his fourth accident, they finally sent him to a detox clinic. I think he's been dry since. I know he still goes to church."

"Does that bother you?"

"I don't know," Mark answered honestly, "but what does bother me is he never acknowledged the accident at all. I tell myself it doesn't matter. It won't bring the baby back. But it would still be nice if he said he was sorry."

Mark's voice cracked again, and he looked so alone, sitting there with his arms folded across bent knees. Julie wanted to share his pain, but knew she couldn't. She wanted him to know it was natural to mourn, to grieve, to cry. Perhaps if she gave him permission. . . .

"If you want to cry now," she said softly, "it's all right with me."

"I don't need to cry," he said stubbornly. "I'm not weak."

"Weak? You endured a life-shattering experience like losing a child without a tear! I'd say that makes you one of the strongest men I know."

Mark didn't answer. He didn't say anything. He didn't think about anything. Suddenly, though, suppressed sorrow erupted from him in uncontrollable sobs. He would never see his daughter grow up, never help her ride a bike, never buy her a pony. He would never send her out on a date or teach her how to drive. He would never give her away at a wedding or bounce her children, his grandchildren, on his knee. And he never got to say goodbye.

It seemed like a long time later that the crying stopped. Mark sniffled a little and wiped his eyes with the back of his hand. He looked over at Julie and hoped she wasn't disgusted.

Wiping away a tear of her own, she smiled gently at him. Mark looked at her sheepishly. "I feel better."

"I thought you might." She smiled at him. "Now tell me about Sadie."

"Tell you about her? I thought I just did."

"No, you told me about you and Denise and Clem," Julie informed him, thinking it revealing that not once had he mentioned the child by name. Maybe it was too painful, but that was before. She cuffed him lovingly on the chin and said, "Now I want to hear about your daughter."

Mark was amazed. So overcome with grief over losing her, he hadn't thought of Sadie herself in a long time. With a wistful smile, he said, "Well, she had blonde curls and big blue eyes. She used to look at me with total, unconditional love. It was great. I always called her my little angel."

He went on to tell Julie that Sadie's first word was "da-da." About how she learned to walk by holding onto Max's tail and waddling along behind him. About how she loved to go for horseback rides in his lap. And all the other things they used to do together. . . . It was almost sundown before he finished.

"Tell me, any more skeletons in your closet?" Julie asked without thinking as they rose to their feet and stretched out their stiff muscles. When she realized what she said, she was mortified. "Oh, I'm so sorry! What a horrible choice of words!"

Mark just laughed and assured her that his closets were clean. "How about yours? Any skeletons there?"

"No great secrets here," she shrugged. "I've told you about my parents and my aunt."

"How about that old boyfriend in New York?"

"Vinny? Oh, he's history, ancient history, I promise."

"Good," Mark replied, taking her face in his hands. After studying it a minute, he whispered coarsely, "Thanks."

"For what?"

"For being there. I miss that little tyke so much, but for once, I feel like life will go on, and maybe I can have another shot at happiness."

Julie wanted to help him find that happiness. She gazed into his blue eyes and found herself lost in their depths. She thought she'd burst for the love she felt.

Mark looked into Julie's brown eyes and knew he was doing what he swore he'd never do again. They leaned together slowly, naturally. Their lips melted into a deep, rewarding kiss. No one on horseback interrupted them. No one peeked through curtains to gossip about them. No one disturbed them at all. And after that, no one spoke of just being friends.

The next evening, Julie got a call from Vonda. Although they spoke weekly, it was always good to hear from her. And tonight, Vonda was in the mood to talk . . . about life in the city, life at Mercy hospital, and life in general. Julie stroked Uncle Sam on the belly as she talked.

"Old Doc Richards told us nurses we didn't know how to handle a confused patient," Vonda chuckled at one point. "So he marched in and told Mr. Petrie to settle down and quit hitting the help. You know what Mr. Petrie did?"

"What?"

"Well, he up and punched Dr. Richards right in the gut. It knocked the wind out of him, and he left the room doubled over and wheezing. We had a good laugh over that."

"Sounds like he deserved it," Julie observed, smiling as the cat began to purr.

"You bet he did! Hey, how is that Mark of yours? Recovering?"

"Yeah, he had his appointment today and the doctor said no heavy farm work for awhile, but a little work around the house is okay."

"Good, and are you two still 'friends'?"

"Of course!"

"You sound as if you're hiding something from me, child!"

"Well. . . ."

Julie couldn't keep a secret from Vonda if she tried. She knew better now, and she told her long-distance friend everything. She ended, "I'm not sure what I want out of the relationship, let alone what Mark wants."

"Well, he sounds a heck of a lot better than Mr. LaRosa," Vonda exclaimed. "If it's meant to be, things will work out. Hey, did I tell you what Fern down in the emergency center said the other day . . ."

When Vonda talked for another half hour, Julie made a mental note to send her some money for the phone bill. She would have to disguise it, however, in the form of a gift. Wasn't her birthday coming up? Yeah, it was the day before Mark's. Julie would have to think of something special to do for him, too. Hmm . . .

Chapter Sixteen

Still prohibited from anything he considered real work—washing dishes didn't count—Mark had a long, boring Saturday. With Julie at work, Sunday promised to be more of the same. Maybe he'd wander down and see if they'd let him help with the morning milking. It couldn't be any harder than doing laundry.

Mark went out the back door, bending to scratch old Max on the head. He paused at the sound of arguing, and more particularly, at Troy's words, "Mark doesn't go to church, and no one bugs him to death about it."

Mark scowled. The words of that stupid little poem came back to haunt him . . . "watchful eyes were all about." He had no idea, all those years ago, that his decision to shun church would sprout seeds like this. Darn that Troy anyway!

Mark knew what he had to do, and he wasn't very happy about it. In fact, he dreaded it more than a root canal. But he took a deep breath and went inside to change. Twenty minutes later, he sauntered over to Steve's house, banging on the back door before he walked inside.

Troy was sitting at the kitchen table in his work clothes, eating cereal. Joyce was at the kitchen sink trying to comb down Thad's rooster tail, and Steve was tying Tommy's necktie. Sarah was there, borrowing aluminum foil for a roast.

They all stared at Mark . . . dressed in church clothes! Ignoring them, Mark walked straight over to Troy and barked, "Get ready for church!"

Troy was as taken back as anyone, but he recovered quickly. "I'm not going." He sounded firm.

"Come here," Mark marched his nephew into the living room. No one meant to eavesdrop, but they couldn't help overhearing. Mark wasn't exactly talking quietly. Frozen, they listened.

"Why not?"

"I'm going water-skiing. Since when do you care anyway?"

"Since you started using me as an excuse."

"I can do what I want!" Troy replied with irritation.

"That's what I always thought . . . I can do what I want," Mark mimicked his nephew. "Well, everything we do has far-reaching effects. Didn't you learn anything from those drugs you took?"

"One time, big deal."

"Yeah, I suppose that's what Clem Watkins said when he drove home that night. A few drinks, big deal. Well, it was a big deal. And his actions had far-reaching effects, didn't they? They had an effect on little Sadie, and they sure as hell had an effect on me!"

Those in the kitchen looked at each other in shock. Mark never spoke of Sadie, nor would he allow anyone else to talk about her either. And he never, ever mentioned Clem Watkins, not in five years. They watched and waited as Mark continued.

"I skipped church for personal reasons, never thinking it would have an effect on you. Well, you can't use me as an excuse anymore, because I'm going to church today. And if I'm going, you're going. So get dressed."

Mark stomped back through the kitchen, scowling at everyone in sight. Families were a pain in the neck. He started the Jeep, not caring a bit if he should drive yet or not. He'd be glad to move to the West farm where he could have some privacy!

Actually, the church meetings weren't half bad. They slipped in during the opening song. Mark started singing, and after an elbow in his ribs, Troy did, too. One of the talks was about the prodigal son, and the other about Alma the younger. Mark didn't need to listen to either, but he paid attention anyway, for Troy's sake.

Mark dragged Troy to Sunday School class, then to priesthood meeting. When they split for classes, he didn't know where to go. Finally, he tagged along with Rick and his deacons.

After the meetings, ward members gathered on the front sidewalk to mingle. Mark tried to slip out unnoticed, but to no avail. The bishop pumped his hand enthusiastically, as did several others. Joyce needed help carrying her visual aids, and LuAnn Frost invited him to Sunday dinner.

Declining tactfully, Mark extracted himself from the clutches of the latter. He couldn't drive away fast enough. Five years ago, he had wanted attention, feeling slighted when it didn't come. Now he was getting more attention than he needed. He wasn't sure which was worse.

"Well, it looks like I'll be owning my own farm," Mark announced Monday during a celebration lunch with Julie at the hospital.

Squeezing his hand across the cafeteria table, she exclaimed, "That's wonderful! It's official?"

"I signed a hundred papers or so, but Standish said the final loan approval would take about six weeks."

"Do you have to wait that long to move in?" Julie teased. "I don't think you can. You look like a kid on Christmas morning."

Mark grinned as he sipped his Pepsi. "Ma said I could move in as soon as it was ready."

"There's a lot to do, but you're on your way," Julie smiled. "When can you get horses?"

"I'll have to fix the corral first."

"Can I help?"

The thought of Julie hammering a nail made Mark smile. He had no doubts she'd get right in there and try. Denise wouldn't. No, she'd sit back and wait for her palace on a silver platter, while Julie would be out there digging the moat.

After Mark agreed to let her help, he asked, innocently enough, "Now the doctor said I can work around the house, right?"

Glancing at her watch, Julie answered absentmindedly, "Yes, he did."

"Well," Mark said slyly, "Maybe I'll do a little housework this afternoon. Meet me at the farm after work?"

"Which farm?"

"Mine!"

Between this and that, it was almost evening before Julie arrived. She nearly died when she saw Mark on a ladder. When he finished scraping that piece of siding, the entire house would be ready for new paint. Several buckets of it sat on the porch beside a pile of rollers, brushes, and dropcloths.

"Hey, Julie! How does it look?" Mark ignored her glare as he climbed down. "I should be able to get the first coat on tomorrow."

"This is your idea of a little housework?" she asked incredulously.

"You bet! Just following doctor's orders. Besides, this can't be work. I'm having too much fun."

"Humph!"

She took Mark by the hand and led him to the front steps where she felt his forehead for fever and peeked at his incision. Mark snorted with exasperation, claiming he never felt better. He did agree to stop long enough to show her around the farm.

The house had started as a log cabin, Mark explained, built by one of the first settlers in Birch Creek, Michael West. The house grew over the years, each new occupant adding a room here or a porch there to fit the needs of their family. All in all, it was in fairly good shape.

The porch was strong without sagging. The spindles in the railing were hand-carved, as was the porch swing. The windows were topped by diamond-shaped leaded glass, and the front door bore an oval-shaped, etched window.

Inside, a wide hallway ran the length of the house, the back door visible at the other end. A wide staircase leading to the second floor sat to the left. The woodwork on the open bannister was dark and scuffed, but well-formed.

"It's so cool in here," Julie exclaimed.

"Literally or figuratively?"

"Both. Is there air-conditioning?"

"No, thick walls," Mark banged on one. "No summer heat in here."

The layout of the house was simple, and the rooms were large and airy with high ceilings. Left of the entryway was a large living room with a brick fireplace filling an entire wall. Across the hall on the right was a large, formal dining room. It had several large, built-in cabinets with glass doors.

Behind the dining room sat a large country kitchen. The cabinets were white with glass doors, and the countertops were blue and white tile. A window above the sink revealed a view of the church. Cuts and scrapes lined a polished butcher's block in the middle of the room.

"This room was actually the original log cabin," Mark told Julie.

Imagine! A whole cabin was only the size of the kitchen. Julie shook her head in disbelief, then stared when Mark told her the original pioneers, Michael and Eugenia West, raised six or seven children there as well.

In the southeast corner of the house behind the kitchen was a sunny breakfast nook. Across the hall sat a small bathroom, a pantry, and a mud room where the smell of the barnyard still lingered. A screened-in porch ran across the back of the house.

Upstairs were several large bedrooms and another bathroom. The old-fashioned tub sat on legs, and the sink on a pedestal. Though the carpets in the bedrooms were worn, the closets were large and there were lots of windows. The bedroom above the kitchen had an excellent view of Angel's Peak, aglow now with light from the setting sun.

Retracing their steps, Mark opened a door near the pantry. They walked down narrow stairs to the basement. It was dark and musty with rough walls and no windows. In the dim glow of a single light bulb, they saw a furnace and laundry area. The rest was filled with shelves for food storage and empty canning jars, the crusty remains of a few spiders inside.

Back in the dining room, Mark asked Julie what she thought of the house.

"I love it," she said enthusiastically. "But you know," she looked around the dining room, "I'd make this room into a family room with those cabinets for an entertainment center."

"Yeah?" Mark was skeptical.

"The breakfast nook would be enough dining area," Julie said, then pointed to the living room across the hall. "And that could be a more formal living room."

Mark looked around and nodded slowly. When he turned back to tell her that he liked it, Julie was gone. He almost tripped over her. She was down on her hands and knees, examining a large hole in the carpet.

"You have hardwood floors under here!"

"So," he shrugged.

"So? Hardwood is a very popular these days. If it were up to me, I'd rip out these carpets."

"What else would you do?" Mark asked, helping her up.

"Well," Julie took him by the hand and led him into the hallway. She pointed to the pantry and the mud room. "I'd make one of these rooms into a laundry room."

"Maybe tear out this wall," Mark added, "and make it into one big room. A laundry room with a sink for cleaning up after chores."

"The windows in here," Julie pointed to the pantry, "would help keep down the smell."

"A vented fan in the wall would help, too," Mark commented. "The plumbing should handle a washer. I'll have to check on wiring for a dryer."

"Speaking of wiring," Julie glanced upward at the small light above them, "you should add some extra lights and plugs."

"You certainly are observant," Mark chuckled. "Rick does some electrical work on the side. I think he'd be willing to help. Anything else?"

"Remove the dark stain on this wood," Julie ran a gentle hand over the bannister. "I'll bet it's oak underneath."

"I thought you always lived in apartments. How do you know so much about homes?"

"Magazines," Julie smiled. "This house has some incredible potential. I can tell I'm going to be busy."

"Busy helping?"

"No, busy keeping you from working too hard."

Mark just laughed.

Over the next few weeks of August, the dog days of summer were in full swing. Sirius, the Dog Star so brilliant in the winter sky, now rose and set undetected with the sun. It was doggone hot, and old Max spent most of his day on the back step of Mark's new house, eyeing Uncle Sam warily.

And Mark and Julie were dog-tired each night after working hard on the farm. They washed, scrubbed, and polished. They painted, scraped, and wired. They mowed, weeded, and trimmed.

With help from Rick, the new laundry room turned out better than anyone expected. The corral was quickly taking shape. There were lights and plugs everywhere. The polished wood floors looked great, and the bannister really was oak!

Mark worked all day, and Julie joined him in the evenings and on her days off. They shared makeshift meals wherever they could find a clean spot. Mark even made caramel popcorn for them one evening in Grandma West's kitchen, using her old recipe.

They ate it in the porch swing. Julie made sure Mark rested there often. When they ended up in each other's arms more than once, Mark began to think resting was worthwhile.

They liked working as a team. They laughed a lot and spent each evening whispering in the moonlight. Though it was unspoken, each understood their shared effort on the house would benefit them both eventually.

Fixing up was followed by furniture. Mark bought a modular sofa for the converted family room. He found an old table in the back of the barn for the breakfast nook. Julie found a dainty Victorian living room set in the attic. They even found Grandma's piano in the back of a closet.

Piece by piece, room by room, the house was becoming a home. Mark didn't set a moving date, though. He wouldn't admit it, but he didn't want to do so without Julie. Every night, he returned to the rambler on Jackson Acres, and Julie returned to her apartment . . . alone.

Julie relished the quiet of the emergency room. With their hectic schedule of late, she hadn't relaxed in weeks. Her shift was about over, and Mark was coming by to drive her to pick up the Explorer from its oil change.

The bell above the door jingled, and Julie looked up expectedly. What made her more irritated? The fact that it wasn't Mark, or the fact that it was Fast Eddie? Grief!

Seeing that she was the only one in the emergency room, he came around the desk and stood much too close to her. "Baby, long time no see!" he crooned.

It had been a while, and Julie had hoped he'd fallen off the planet. Or at least, forgotten she existed. But here he was, as slick as ever. Instinctively, she backed up, "What do you want?"

"You really want to know, baby?" Eddie whispered hotly.

He reeked of alcohol. Grabbing a chair, Julie held it between Eddie and herself. She had done this quick-step with him before. With a frown, she demanded, "If you're here on official business, name it. If not, leave!"

"I'd love to have business with you, official or not." Eddie winked provocatively.

Julie didn't know whether to laugh or be sick. He probably thought he was appealing, but he was pathetic. Eddie tried to grab her, but she jumped beyond his reach, nearly falling over a stretcher in the process.

"I don't have time or energy for this stupid game today."

"Quit playing hard to get, then, and come over here."

He was around the stretcher in seconds. Julie bolted. Eddie was right behind her, oozing insincere compliments as he reached out and grabbed her. Julie struggled, but he was faster than he looked. And stronger, too!

"Get out of my emergency room!" Julie shrieked as Eddie ran his hands through her hair, then pulled her close, pinning her arms down at her sides.

"Come on, baby. You know you want it," he hinted lustfully, rubbing his thumbs up and down her arms. "I've heard about you. Heard that you do this sort of thing all the time. Talk is you're a regular trollop. A trollop, ha! What old biddy came up with that name?!"

Mrs. Ellsberg, Julie thought with a shudder as she resisted his unwanted advances. Eddie made all sorts of lewd suggestions, and she twisted and turned to pry herself from his grasp. Neither of them heard the bell over the door.

"Get your hands off her now!" Mark bellowed, grabbing Eddie by the shoulder and pulling him away. Julie went sprawling across the room. With shaking hands, she grasped the desk for support.

"Aw, leave us alone, Marko buddy. We're just having fun."

"It didn't look like Julie was having fun. Were you having fun, Julie?"

She didn't trust her voice, so she merely shook her head and wiped her eyes with the back of her hand. With that, Mark was furious. He resisted an urge to take her into his arms immediately. There was something he had to do first. He turned back to Eddie with a murderous glare.

"Don't you ever touch her again," Mark declared through

clenched teeth, "or you'll be answering to me."

"You're making time with the hussy, too, man?"

That was it. Mark punched Eddie square on the jaw, and at the same time, released his grip on his shoulder. The force of the blow sent Eddie tumbling across the room. He landed sideways over a stretcher, and there he stayed.

Julie was in Mark's arms instantly. She buried her face in his leather jacket. He smoothed her hair and held her tight. "Are you okay?" His voice was gentle. She looked up at him, her eyes brimming with tears, and Mark gently wiped them away.

He was overcome with a protective feeling towards Julie. In fact, he wanted to spend the rest of his life protecting her from cads like Eddie, from tears and heartache, from loneliness. There was only one way he knew of doing that. He knew he'd have to hurry before he lost his nerve.

"I'm fine now," Julie managed to say at last.

"Let's get out of here then," he suggested, unmindful of the nurses, the doctor, and the volunteers who came running to see what happened. "We've got to talk."

Chapter Seventeen

"Julie?" Mark said softly as they held hands in the porch swing later that evening.

"Yes?" she replied, thinking she knew what he wanted to say and wondering what was taking him so long.

"Uh," he hesitated, "I was wondering. . . ."

He leaned forward, looked intently at a hangnail, and felt every ounce of nerve drain from him. This was hard! The setting didn't seem right earlier in the Jeep or at the service station. Once Julie arrived at the West farm, they were too busy.

And now? He was chickening out! If only there was some sort of guarantee that things would work this time. Julie wasn't Denise, but doubts crept in anyway. What if she hated country life after all? What if she pressured him about the Church? What if they ended up fighting all the time? What if? What if?

". . . Uh, wondering if you want to go out Saturday night? It's my birthday, you know, so I thought we could go someplace special. There's this little restaurant in Logan Canyon with an outdoorsy atmosphere . . . Pine something. I've heard it's romantic."

"Romantic, huh?" Julie smiled as Mark kissed her fingertips. "How can I resist that?"

What else could she say that wouldn't make him suspicious? She wasn't going to let anything ruin the surprise birthday party. She and Debbie had been planning it for weeks. And with the help of Sarah and Annie, everyone Mark knew was going to be there.

Rocking back and forth in silence, each became lost in their own thoughts. Julie was figuring out how to get Mark to the surprise party. And Mark was convincing himself that in the ideal setting of the restaurant, he would ask Julie to be his bride.

Julie cursed for the first time in months as she surveyed the pathetic results of her latest attempt to make Mark's birthday present. She had an idea, a piece of pottery with different colors of clay to form the shape of Angel's Peak. It wasn't working out.

Mark loved her pottery. And she'd been hinting all week that he was going to love her present. The party was tonight, though, and time was running out. Could she give him one of her old pieces? No, it needed to be something more special.

Glancing at her watch, she saw it was time to pick up his cake from the bakery. She threw her last-ditch effort into the huge heap of discards in the corner. From his favorite place atop the television, Uncle Sam watched calmly as she stomped out the door.

As she hurried toward the bakery, the needed gift was still on Julie's mind. A small set of scriptures in a passing window caught her eye, but she only laughed. That would be the last thing on earth she would get Mark for his birthday. He would hate them!

As she returned down the sidewalk with the cake in hand, Julie saw the scriptures again. Once again, she pushed the notion aside. Tucking the cake into the back of the Explorer, she looked around. Now to find a present! She had less than ten minutes.

The scriptures beckoned to her. She walked over to the bookstore and peered inside. Mark would hate them. Well, he was going to church these days. He still didn't want to talk about it, though. Precious seconds ticked away. Oh, what should she do?

Julie uttered a quick, silent prayer, asking that very question of the Lord. Never before was she hit with such a swift and forceful answer. *Get the scriptures.* Oh, she hoped he'd understand.

The store smelled like a library, and the man behind the counter looked like an old librarian, glasses perched upon his nose and black bands at the elbows of his white shirt. He praised

Julie on her excellent choice. The books were bound in leather, and the lettering was real, 14-karat gold.

"Now do you want a name engraved on them? It's free."

"That would be great," Julie hesitated, "but is there time?"

"I can whip it up in no time," he assured her. When Julie handed him a card with the name printed on it, he chuckled, "Ah, little Markie Jackson, huh? He used to come in here all the time wanting Article of Faith cards. I think he and his friends used 'em for trading cards."

That made Julie feel better. Maybe Mark wouldn't hate them so bad, after all. She thanked the man for his help and ran from the store as soon as the books were ready.

Back at the apartment, Julie took the time to write a message in each volume before she wrapped them. Inside the Bible, she wrote a happy birthday message to Mark, noting the date and drawing a funny little picture of balloons. Inside the Book of Mormon, she wrote her testimony.

Donning the latest from Stella—a colorful dress of flowered silk, Julie ran a comb through her hair. Then grabbing her things, she dashed to the Explorer. Uncle Sam waved goodbye from the window, but Julie didn't have time to scold him. She could only hope that Mrs. Ellsberg wouldn't notice.

Julie had concocted a reason to meet Mark at the West farm, calling to say she'd found the perfect wreath for his new front door. Though she had yet to reach the speed limit, Julie made it there in record time. She even stopped at Jackson Acres to drop off the cake and her present.

Everything was ready. The guests were beginning to arrive, but there wasn't a car was in sight. Everyone parked down the road, and Troy, Gary, and Woody transported them to Sarah's on four-wheelers. Even Grandma Parsons enjoyed the ride.

Mark was waiting in the porch swing when Julie arrived at the farm. He looked nice in gray slacks and a tweed jacket. She greeted him with a big kiss and hug, then presented the wreath for his approval.

“That’s nice,” he said, smiling, “but do we have to hang it right away?”

Julie simply nodded, so Mark carefully hammered a nail into the wood above the oval window. When Julie placed the wreath on the nail, it hung at a funny angle off the rim of the window. Mark had an idea for that, using a loop of fishing line so it rested evenly against the glass. Perfect!

“Now, let’s go,” Mark dragged her to the car.

As they neared Jackson Acres, Julie said, “Oh, I need to stop a minute. Sarah had me bring a prescription for her.”

Mark scowled, but pulled into the graveled drive. “Just don’t take too long. It’s a weekend, and the restaurant will be crowded.”

She needed Mark to go in with her . . . think quick! “Oh, your mother said Robyn is in labor. Let’s see if she’s had the baby yet. It’ll only take a minute, I promise.”

As they approached the door, Julie was certain she heard “They’re here!” and “Shh!” and “Everybody hide!” filtering out. She glanced quickly at Mark. He seemed clueless. She had no idea that he was hoping they could get to Logan so he could pop the question before he turned coward again.

Opening the door, Julie called inside, “Sarah! We’re here!”

Pandemonium broke loose as soon as Mark stepped in after her. People came out of the woodwork. Some were calling out “Surprise!” and “Happy Birthday!” while others blew little horns or threw balloons and streamers around Sarah’s crowded living room.

Mark was dumbfounded. It took him a minute to understand what was going on. He’d never had a surprise party in his life! Did Julie know about this? He looked over, and she was grinning ear to ear. *That little scamp,* he thought with affection and burst out laughing.

Julie sighed with relief. She knew Mark was looking forward to dinner in Logan, and she had hoped he wouldn’t be too upset. When he took her in his arms and lovingly threatened to get even, she knew everything would be okay.

In the next hour, Mark was greeted by everyone he knew—immediate family, distant relatives, neighbors, ward members, friends from his youth, and even faculty members from school. Some people he hadn't seen for ages. *How did Julie manage to pull this off?* He looked toward her and she answered him with a smile.

As the party progressed, Tommy snapped pictures with a Polaroid. As the photographs developed, they all guessed who would appear. There was Steve yawning, Thad's fingers in the icing, and Sarah on the phone. Everyone's favorite was Mark and Julie stealing a kiss.

After the cake, but before the presents, Sarah came out and announced that Robyn just called. The baby was here, and it was another boy! Mark took the joking about sharing his birthday good-naturedly.

He couldn't say that about everything he'd heard that night. Quite honestly, he was frustrated over another delay in his plans. And given more time to think about it, he was beginning to feel panicked.

The gossip around made him feel pressured. Bishop Owens was telling everyone that he had introduced the happy couple. Aunt Vergie, ninety years old and deaf as a post, asked Sarah when the wedding would be. And even Grandma Parsons couldn't leave it alone.

Mark just had to open the presents on the piano, then he could make his escape. And hopefully, take Julie with him. Maybe in the quiet of the night, he could muster enough nerve to ask her. Then again, maybe not!

Mark chuckled at the designer toilet paper from Rick and Annie, admired the paperweight Thad made from a rock, and whistled at the knitted scarf from Grandma Parsons. The rest of the gifts weren't much better. He couldn't wait to open his last gift, the one from Julie.

As she handed it to him, he returned her sheepish smile with a wink. It felt heavy. She'd told him it was going to be special, that he was going to love it. He had an idea what she meant. Eagerly, he tore off the wrappings, then peered inside. It wasn't the Julie Craig original pottery piece he had expected. It was *scriptures,* of all things.

When his face dropped, so did Julie's heart. Troy's laughter or Sarah's exclamations of joy didn't help. He tried to hide his disappointment behind half-hearted words of thanks, but Julie knew. He hated them, just like she feared. Why did the Spirit tell her to buy them, anyway?

As Annie jumped up to fill the strained silence with parlor games, Mark tossed the box aside and went out the back door. Hoping she wouldn't burst into tears, Julie followed him. They met in the darkened yard, neither speaking as they watched a silvery moon rise over the horizon.

Finally, Julie said meekly, "I'm sorry you hated my gift so much."

"Well, what did you expect? All week, you promised something great, something I would love. Scriptures, Julie? Really."

"The scriptures are great," she countered. "Maybe you should try reading them sometime."

"I've read in them," he claimed. "No big deal."

"Reading in them," Julie returned with feeling, "and reading them are two different things. You have to read with the right spirit, and if you prayerfully ask for it, you'll get a witness they're true."

"Oh sure," Mark said sarcastically, never quite believing that. It was just one of those things seminary teachers said.

"Why don't you just try it?"

"I'm not ready," Mark bellowed. "Don't pressure me."

"Don't pressure me, don't pressure me," Julie mimicked with irritation. The strain was getting to her. She was tired . . . from long hours at his house, from planning his party, and of dealing with his ever-changing moods. "I have bent over backwards not to pressure you."

"You call giving me scriptures no pressure?"

"I walk on eggshells around you when it comes to the Church, but I'm tired of it. The Church means a lot to me, and I can't pretend it doesn't just because you might feel pressured."

"You don't have to walk on eggshells anymore," Mark threw up his hands in defeat, "because I'm out of here."

"Running away again?"

"I never run away from my problems."

"Maybe not physically, but emotionally you run like the dickens!"

Mark swung around, glaring fiercely, "What do you mean by that?"

"Take this church thing, for example. You think a few people in the Church treated you badly, so you run away and blame us all. The Church isn't a club of perfect people, you know, it's a clinic of those willing to improve themselves."

"I'd call them a bunch of hypocrites. What ever happened to love your neighbor and do unto others?"

"And you're any better?" Julie asked in a low voice. "Going to church with Troy even though you don't believe in it or care a thing about it?"

Mark didn't answer, though a muscle twitched madly in his clenched jaw. Julie took advantage of his silence to go on, "I think you blame your attitude about the Church on the way the people of Birch Creek acted five years ago when you actually never bothered to get a testimony of your own."

"Yeah? What difference would that make anyway?"

Julie couldn't believe him. "A lot of difference. Your eternal soul is at stake. Can't you see that you need the Church?"

Mark knew he was being stubborn, but why couldn't Julie accept him as he was? Why were people always trying to make him into some sort of a spiritual giant? Then a thought struck . . .was it really them, or was it him? Did he have some underlying need to get in harmony with his religious upbringing? Nonsense!

"I don't need any of them," Mark declared, referring to members of the Church in general and members of the Birch Creek Ward in particular.

"When you say 'them' you're including me," Julie choked with emotion, "because I'm a Mormon. If you can't accept them, you can't accept me."

She ended her declaration with a bit of a question in her voice. This whole thing sounded too much like her last conversation with Vinny. Why did she always have to choose between love and the Church? Was it a test of her faith? Was she too inflexible? Couldn't she ever have both?

Mark didn't answer right away. Half of him wanted to take Julie in his arms and kiss away the tears he heard in her voice. The other half knew he couldn't live a lie. And pretending that he accepted the Church would be a lie, plain and simple.

"I can't pretend to accept something for which I have no feelings." He sounded hesitant.

Mark was referring to the Church, but in the pain of the moment Julie didn't realize that. Did he mean he had no feelings for her? That it had all been a farce? A joke? Something to distract him during the long, boring summer? Her heart shattered into a million pieces, and she could hold back the tears no longer.

"I guess this means goodbye then," Julie muttered and ran from the yard, peeling out with gravel flying before Mark could stop her.

Should he follow? And then what, continue the argument somewhere else? The angry words and unresolved conflict reminded him of life with Denise. Would things end up the same with Julie? Up until now, he'd have said "no." They'd never fought before.

So was this a foreshadowing of the future? If so, maybe it was better that he didn't ask her to marry him. He couldn't go through another relationship like that, no matter how much he thought of the girl. Oh, to heck with her. To heck with all of them!

Mark stomped over to the house where he'd lived alone for five years. Maybe he just wasn't cut out for love and marriage and happiness. He'd survived before, and he could do it again. Then a cold, hard fact slapped him in the face. Getting over Julie wasn't going to be anything like getting over Denise!

"Hey, Mark," a voice called out to him from the darkness. It was Bishop Owens. "I've been looking all over for you. Got a favor to ask."

Mark sounded as bleak as he felt. "Shoot."

"The big boys in Boise have called a special session next week to discuss next year's funding for education. We need some educators up there to represent our interests."

"Yeah?" Mark knew what was coming and refused to offer.

"I'll be up there all week myself. The superintendent and some of the school board are going for a day or two. The elementary school is sending a couple of teachers. I'm trying to round up some of mine to go, too."

"And you wondered if I'd spend the week in Boise?"

"Well, as much of it as you can. Steve said you can't help on the farm yet, so I figured you'd have the time."

"Well. . . ." Mark hesitated. Time wasn't the problem. As it was, time was going to hang heavy on his hands for awhile.

"Your mother told me about the place you're fixing up. If you're just too busy, I'll understand."

Mark thought about the West farm. Half the fun of being there was working side by side with Julie. Maybe spending time in Boise, miles away from all the things that reminded him of her, would be just the thing he needed. Mark agreed to go for the whole week.

"Great!" Bishop Owens exclaimed. "You can drive up with me then. In fact, the wife's folks have an extra bed you can use."

"Driving together sounds good." Mark had wondered if the old Jeep would make it that far. "But I'd rather stay in a motel, if you don't mind."

Mark didn't want company. He wanted to be alone. He

wanted to spend free time from meetings in quiet misery, not thinking about Julie . . . not thinking about anything. He felt the fibers of another cocoon closing in around him.

Chapter Eighteen

The next day, Julie was in a blue mood. She couldn't go anywhere or do anything that didn't remind her of Mark. Even in sacrament meeting, she spent the whole time mentally reviewing their final words about the Church. She wanted to get her bishop's advice about the whole situation, but as luck would have it, Bishop Owens was out of town.

She took Uncle Sam for a drive that afternoon, instinctively heading for Birch Creek. Mark's Jeep wasn't at Jackson Acres or the West farm, but she didn't notice or care . . . not in the least. She drove over Snow Canyon to Bear Lake and spent an hour telling herself that the blue, blue water wasn't the color of Mark's eyes!

As she drove home, she wondered about this unofficial mission of hers in Oakwood. Weeks ago, she thought it might be to find love, but now she was confused. Why Oakwood? Why Mark? Why scriptures? Why? Why? Why? All questions, no answers.

The following day, Julie prayed for a busy day at work. She wanted to keep her hands and mind busy. She didn't want to think of Mark . . . of the times he visited here, of the night he had appendicitis, of when he punched Fast Eddie out, of anything that reminded her of him.

The morning was slow. The first patient of the day, a man with a laceration on his leg from a minor car accident, arrived about ten-thirty. Dr. Bolinsky came over from his office to stitch him up. Sheriff Porter was there, too, questioning the injured about the wreck.

In the thick of things, Julie scarcely noticed Kathleen Ward come into the room. The director of nursing smiled apologetically as she handed Julie a small yellow piece of paper. A telegram! With trembling hands, Julie opened it, gasping as she read:

VONDA COLLAPSED THIS AM. AT MERCY. STOP.
FERN

"Not Vonda," Julie whispered as she rose to her feet. But her legs were shaking and she sat down again with a dazed look. The message was too brief. Was Vonda ill? Dying? Dead?

Everyone looked at everyone else as they tried to figure out what had happened. Dr. Bolinsky broke the spell. "What is it? Bad news?"

"My friend . . . collapsed . . . I don't know what's wrong . . . I've got to go to New York . . . I've got to go now!"

"Well, you go then," Kathleen replied. "I'll fill in here until I can find a replacement. I don't think my nursing skills are too rusty."

Dr. Bolinsky had finished with the suturing. He picked up the phone. "I'll arrange a flight for you, Julie. Salt Lake to La Guardia okay?"

"Sure," Julie mumbled with an incoherent nod.

"You don't look like you're in shape to drive anywhere, young lady," the sheriff noted. "I'll take you over to your place so you can pack, then drive you to the airport myself. I don't want to be scraping you off the side of the road. You ready to go?"

Julie's heart was fluctuating between fear for Vonda and gratitude for the kindness of her friends. She smiled gratefully. "How can I ever thank you all?"

"No problem," Sheriff Porter replied. "In small towns, we take care of our own."

Those words made Julie want to cry, but she didn't. Her eyes stayed dry, and she felt oddly detached from the whole situation.

Was she packing? Was she taking her cat over to Debbie's? Was she calling Mercy? Did she get lost in a jumble of operators? Did she even try to call Mark? Oh, what would he care anyway?

As they drove to Salt Lake City, Julie thought about her arrival some five months ago. It seemed like yesterday, but so much had happened since then—both good and bad. Maybe coming to Idaho was a mistake. Maybe the feeling she experienced when making the decision was only indigestion. Maybe she'd send for Uncle Sam and stay in New York.

About the time Julie's flight landed in New York, Mark was opening his suitcase in his motel room in Boise. As he rummaged around for something comfortable to wear, he realized he wouldn't make a good politician. Meetings were for the birds!

Mark's hand brushed against something hard. *What in the world?* He pulled out the Book of Mormon Julie had given him. Resisting the urge to throw it across the room, he dug a little deeper in his suitcase and pulled out the Bible. *How did those get in there?* he thought in disgust.

Ma! When Mark did his laundry at her house, he had asked her to pack a few things for him from the dryer. She must have packed the books, too. Good grief! Could he never get away from these high-pressure pests who wanted to save his soul?

There was a St. Louis Cardinals baseball game on T.V. so he set the scriptures aside, unwrapped his hamburger, and settled in. In the second inning, it started raining. An hour later, it was still coming down in buckets, so the game was called off. Mark flipped off the television with disgust. The silence was deafening.

He looked around for something to read. Even brochures from the Chamber of Commerce were better than twiddling his thumbs. Then he noticed the scriptures waiting patiently on the nightstand. There was nothing else to read. He picked up the Book of Mormon.

Flipping casually through it, the words looked like the same dry passages he'd avoided reading in seminary. What was so great about this? Maybe he should read it and pray about it just to prove Julie wrong. When he didn't get a witness from the Spirit, he could tell them all to leave him alone once and for all.

Julie was frantic by the time she arrived at Mercy Hospital. The ride from the airport in a filthy cab had taken forever. Even Mark's muddy Jeep was never this bad, she thought as she tried to make as little contact with the seat as possible.

She ran into the emergency room, glad to catch Fern at the end of her twelve-hour shift. The latter was just clocking out when Julie exclaimed breathlessly, "I came as soon as I could."

"Why, Craig," the redhead looked surprised, "I had no idea you'd come when I sent that telegram. Vonda has no family, you know. I got your hospital's address from old personnel files. I knew you'd kept in touch, so I thought I'd let you know."

Julie nodded. "I'm glad you did. What happened?"

"Diabetic reaction, from what I heard. It was so sudden. One minute she was sitting at the nurse's desk, the next she was on the floor."

Julie didn't even know that Vonda was diabetic. She dreaded her next question, "Is she . . . uh . . . you know?"

"She's in the medical intensive care unit. Stable now, they say. I went up at lunch, and she looked pretty good."

"Oh, thank goodness." Julie sighed with relief. "Thanks for letting me know, Fern. I owe you one."

Minutes later, Julie was at Vonda's side, stroking the woman's leathery hand as she whispered encouraging words for her friend to get better. Monitors flashed and beeped, but Vonda looked restful. Julie uttered yet one more prayer in her behalf.

As she said "Amen," the older woman's eyes fluttered open. She blinked twice when she saw Julie, then in a raspy whisper, said, "Hello, child. Am I hallucinating?"

"No, Vonda, I'm really here."

"How come? Somebody die?"

"No," Julie wiped away a tear of joy, the first she'd shed during this whole ordeal, "and they had better not either! Why didn't you tell me you have diabetes?"

"Diabetes? I do? Well, what do you know about that?"

Two days later, Vonda was moved to the medical-diabetic floor. And two days after that, after learning about diet, exercise, insulin injections, and how to recognize another reaction, she was discharged. Julie fussed over her the entire time.

As Julie helped Vonda settle back into her small apartment, they talked, mostly about Mark. As usual, Julie told her everything. Vonda was rather quiet as she listened, humming and hawing at all the appropriate moments. Finally, Julie said, "I must be wearing you out with all this nonsense."

"On the contrary," Vonda shook her head. "I find it very interesting. Go on."

"So he told me to quit pressuring him about the Church. Tell me honestly, Vonda, have I ever pressured you about the Church? I mean, I always thought I was open-minded, letting people believe as they may."

"Your beliefs are strong, child, but I've never felt pressured. Then again, you weren't planning on living out your days with me either. Maybe you're trying harder with Mark 'cuz you have more at stake."

"Maybe," Julie sighed, "but it's water under the bridge, I'm afraid. We both said some pretty hateful things when we parted. I'm sure that it's too late for anything more between us now."

"It's never too late, child," Vonda paused. "I was going to say, until you're dead and buried, but y'all believe in living forever, so I'll leave it at never."

Julie rose slowly to her feet, wishing she could believe that. "I'm going to be late for my lunch with Stella. Want anything at the market?"

"Maybe some sugar-free Jello," her friend teased. "Yum, yum! I can't get enough of that stuff."

Julie was laughing as she slipped out into the stale-smelling hallway. When she heard Vonda quickly chain the door behind her, her smile faded. Amazingly enough, she'd grown used to Oakwood where some people didn't even lock their doors at all. New York as a whole seemed like a different planet now. Could she really move back here again?

As she walked down the crowded sidewalk to the subway station, she felt like a stranger. The noise seemed unbearable, as did the filth in the streets and the stagnant heat. Oh, it was vaguely familiar, but it didn't feel like home. Like it or not, her heart was in Idaho.

It was a thought she repeated after her visit with Stella. This lunch was the only time her aunt had all week in her busy schedule to see Julie. That really wasn't surprising, Julie thought as she studied Stella across the tiny table in the posh downtown restaurant. Her aunt hadn't changed much in the last few months. Her hair was still bleached blonde, her nails long and tapered to perfection, her skirts a touch too short. She spent the majority of their time together talking about herself. Julie listened patiently as she related all sorts of stories about her gallery, her limo driver, her latest shopping spree in Paris.

The rest of the time, Stella tried to convince Julie to return to "civilization." She used every argument possible, even telling her niece that she'd heard Vinny LaRosa was still available. Julie simply shook her head and insisted upon returning to Oakwood at the end of the week. She couldn't tell her aunt why—she wasn't really sure herself.

At last, Stella checked her watch and declared it was time to go. Julie followed her into the street, then took the subway back to Vonda's apartment. She almost died when she saw who was seated across the aisle from her—Vinny LaRosa and his mother! They didn't seem to recognize her, but dressed in jeans and a T-shirt without a stitch of makeup, she wasn't surprised.

She found it fun to watch them unobserved. Mama LaRosa was as imposing as ever, with her extra-long cigarette and bright red lipstick. Vinny, however, seemed scrawnier than Julie remembered. But then, she was comparing his swarthy looks to one very tall, rather blondish, and well-built farmer.

In fact, how had she ever thought Vinny handsome? She shook her head in wonder. His nose was too large, his smile too flashy. And his voice? It sounded downright wimpy as he agreed with everything his mother said. *Still tied to her apron-strings,* Julie thought as she quickly and quietly slipped off the train.

The first thing she saw on the platform was a Pepsi machine. The red and blue can that dropped into the tray in response to her coins reminded her of Mark. He always had one close at hand, especially since they started working on the West farm.

Julie sighed at memories of that. Had he finished his corral? Had he gotten any horses yet? Had school started? Were his new students as horrible as he feared? She'd been gone almost a week. Had he missed her even the tiniest bit at all?

At last, she admitted what she had denied all week. She missed him, missed him terribly. Thoughts of him mingled with visions of Vinny on the subway. As she slowly walked back to Vonda's, sipping on the soda, she found herself comparing the two of them objectively.

One difference stood out like a sore thumb. Vinny had never been willing to accept Julie for what she was—a Mormon. And since she was not willing to give that up, things went downhill fast between them.

But Mark, dear sweet Mark, was willing to accept her, all of her. He didn't ask her to quit attending church, but even went with her at times. He never gave her an ultimatum. He had been willing to love her anyway.

All he asked was to be accepted as well, not pressured or prodded to become her idea of the perfect man. He wanted to be accepted for what he was—a kind, thoughtful, and fun-loving guy. Even if he wasn't active in the Church, whatever the reason, he had something to offer Julie. He could bring her great happiness. Wasn't that enough?

He'd claimed to have no feelings for her, but deep down inside, she knew better. She could see it in his eyes. She could feel it in his touch. She could hear it in his tender words. Maybe he didn't even realize it, but he did have feelings for her. Maybe someday those feelings could turn to love. Yes, that would be enough.

Julie was whistling when she reached Vonda's apartment. She gave her startled friend a hug, then walked over to the phone. She dialed Mark's number and reversed the charges to her account.

"Who you calling, child?"

"Mark," Julie replied as if there really was no other answer.

"You going to kiss and make up with him?"

"I'm going to try." Julie wondered why he didn't answer.

"What changed your mind?"

"Believe it or not, Vinny LaRosa! I saw him on the subway and decided that life with Mark, church or not, was better than life alone."

"Or life with a spoiled rotten mama's boy," her friend chuckled. "Well, maybe that LaRosa feller was good for something after all."

There were several flaws in Mark's plan to prove Julie wrong about the Book of Mormon. His first downfall came when he paused long enough to read her inscriptions. He laughed at her drawing of balloons, then traced a reflective finger over the date she had written . . . the day he planned to ask her to marry him, the day he lost her. There was a lump in his throat.

Then he read her testimony inside the Book of Mormon. Subdued, he saw it with different eyes than he would have last week. She spoke from her heart, and the words she used weren't high-pressure or demanding. They were sweet and sincere. Hmm . . .

His second downfall came when two of Tommy's Polaroid pictures fell out of the Bible. Ma's work as well, he thought as he looked them over. One picture was of Julie alone. She looked like she was having the time of her life as she lit the candles on his cake. Mark swallowed hard.

It was a good picture, but it didn't quite bring out the details Mark remembered so well. Like the way she scrunched up her nose when she was disgusted. Or the way she pushed her hair back from her face. Or the sweet scent of her perfume. Or the way she really looked in silk.

The other picture was the one where they were kissing. Julie had leaned over to whisper something in his ear, and Mark had surprised her. Mark's stomach tightened at the memory of kissing Julie.

His final and most fatal downfall was that he actually paid attention as he read. *Can't really disprove her theory if I don't give it a good effort,* he told himself. And he was really surprised that the scriptures were fairly interesting. Oh, he fell asleep during a few chapters, but for the most part, he was intrigued.

He was fascinated with the stories of battles, the stories of faithful prophets, and the repeated stories of pride and apostasy. He couldn't believe people could be so blind. Julie's phrase "Can't you see?" rang through his mind. He was humbled.

By Friday evening, as he read the last few chapters of Moroni, Mark's faltering testimony had grown in leaps and bounds. Like the seedlings of corn Julie trampled upon, it was all the stronger for his painful past. He knew that the Lord still loved him, and even if everyone else turned their back on him, he wasn't alone.

His earlier resolve forgotten, Mark got down on his knees and really prayed. He really wanted to know if the Book of Mormon was true. He felt inadequate, forgetting all the fancy language to use. So he just humbly asked for the witness promised by Moroni.

His answer didn't come with fireworks or visions, but with the most peaceful feeling of warmth. His doubts simply melted away. He knew the Book of Mormon was true. And subsequently, he knew that the Church was true, with the Savior at its head and a living prophet at its headquarters.

Mark prayed again, this time for forgiveness. He promised to try to be a better person, to not judge others, and to render service whenever possible. He asked for the courage to do what he knew—deep down inside—was right. And once again, a sweet feeling of peace entered his soul. He might not be perfect by tomorrow, but he was on the right road. It felt good.

As he knelt there with his head on the edge of the bed, he decided that it was time to get on with life. No more cocoons. It was time to forgive the people of Birch Creek for their actions. Perhaps he even felt sorry for them, caught up in trivial things to the point they couldn't reach out to those in need.

Mark wondered about Clem. Could he forgive him? Clem seemed less like a villain now, and more like a lost soul in the mist of darkness like in Lehi's dream. Releasing the anger and bitterness for him would almost be refreshing. It wouldn't happen overnight, but it was time to start.

At last, Mark rose to his feet, and his eyes fell upon the Polaroid pictures of Julie. He studied them long and hard, then closed his eyes tightly. He was afraid that he had really blown it this time. He'd let his temper get the best of him . . . again.

Hoping it wasn't too late, he reached over and picked up the phone. A hundred rings or so later, he put it down again. Oh, he hoped like anything that he wasn't too late.

Chapter Nineteen

Due to unavoidable delays, Bishop Owens couldn't leave Boise until early Sunday morning. Mark was chomping at the bit by then. Julie hadn't answered her phone all weekend. They reached Oakwood in pretty good time, and he set out at once find her. He had some apologizing to do.

Retrieving his Jeep from the high school parking lot, he swung by her apartment. When he saw both her Explorer and her bicycle there, he relaxed. She couldn't go far without wheels. No one answered his repeated knocking, though, at her or Debbie's door.

Before he could leave the complex, Mark was nearly knocked over as Mrs. Ellsberg literally burst from her apartment, cackling, "Mark!"

He nodded briefly. "Mrs. Ellsberg."

"I suppose you're looking for Julie Craig."

It didn't take a genius to figure that out. He flashed a tight-lipped smile. "Do you know where she is?"

"I haven't seen her all week," the old woman confided importantly. "Rent was due Tuesday, the first. It's the sixth today, and I haven't seen her or her check."

That didn't sound like Julie. Mark frowned as Mrs. Ellsberg continued, "My guess is she skipped out of town. Maybe she had something to hide, if you know what I mean."

"Hardly." Mark's brow furrowed with disdain.

"But I suppose this isn't anything new for you, though, Mark," Mrs. Ellsberg tried to look sympathetic, but actually appeared more smug. "This isn't the first time someone's disappeared on you, now is it?"

Mark barely held his tongue until he reached the Jeep. He wasn't totally a new man yet, and he had a hard time feeling much brotherly love for the likes of Lavon Ellsberg. Her cutting tongue and wicked ways made old Clem look like a saint.

Mark headed to the hospital next. Someone with a pink jacket and a beeper manned the emergency room desk while the regular nurse was on break. It wasn't the best arrangement, but it was Sunday on a holiday weekend. Mark frowned when the volunteer turned. It was LuAnn Frost.

"Hi, Mark," she beamed, hoping her new position would impress him. She knew that was why Julie attracted his attention. It had to be. The snotty girl from New York was nothing special.

He didn't have time for LuAnn. "Do you know where Julie might be?" he asked abruptly.

"Haven't you heard?" LuAnn replied with an air of importance. "Julie went back to New York."

"New York?" he asked incredulously. "When?"

"Monday morning. She just up and left."

Mark's heart skipped a beat, and his stomach dropped considerably. "Are you sure?" he whispered.

"Oh, yes. Everyone's talking about it. There's a lot of speculation about why she went, but no one knows for sure."

"I don't believe it!" He turned and walked slowly toward the door.

LuAnn didn't miss his forlorn expression. "Listen, if you need someone to talk to . . ." she called out after him.

Mark didn't hear the rest. He was wrestling with his thoughts and emotions as he drove away. This couldn't be happening again, could it? Not now—not like this!

He tried to deny it. Julie wouldn't leave her Explorer. She loved it! But didn't she say there was no need for a car in New York? He supposed it was the same with her bike. He was afraid there was no denying it. Julie was gone. The city had won again!

Then why did she claim to love country life so much? Was the allure of the city too great to resist? Was her old boyfriend back in the picture? Why did she have to leave now? Why not a week from now? Why did this always happen when he risked his heart? Why couldn't he fall for someone who wouldn't run off to the . . . the city?

Mark felt drained by the time he reached Jackson Acres. As he unpacked the Jeep, he found that he couldn't quit yawning. Finally, he sought rest on the sofa. Seeking comfort for the pain in his heart, he opened the opened the Book of Mormon and read a chapter or two in Moroni.

Words of faith and miracles struck home. It would take a miracle to get Julie back. Did he have enough faith? Then a sobering thought surfaced. What if Julie wasn't supposed to be a part of his life?

What if she came to Idaho just long enough to give him a Book of Mormon and encourage him to read it? And with that accomplished, what if she was then allowed, by the Spirit, to go back? Mark didn't want to consider that. It ripped away his hope and made his future look bleak.

Mark yawned again. Weeks of work and a week of worry now left him completely spent. Before long, he was sound asleep. He awoke with a start, blinking as he looked around the familiar room in a daze. He felt his lower abdomen for the scar from his surgery.

It was merely a pink strip of healing flesh now. Only a moment ago, it had been covered with gauze and hurt like the dickens. It had to be a dream, but it seemed so real. Were the events in his dream real? Perhaps his forgotten memories about the day of his surgery?

Real or not, Mark knew what he had to do. After stowing a few things into the back of the Jeep, Mark stopped by Sarah's house to tell her his plans. She was speechless . . . absolutely speechless!

Julie left the Salt Lake airport in the passenger seat of Chip Ventura's eighteen-wheeler. She had called Oakwood earlier to see if Debbie could possibly come down and get her. Her friend would be in Malad, but she offered the services of her husband, since he'd be returning from a run to Phoenix on Sunday anyway.

Julie readily accepted the offer, and the ensuing ride was a pleasant one. When they finally rolled into Pine Valley, she sighed contentedly. She felt like she was home at last. She could never live in the city again. The masses there had been celebrating Labor Day all weekend long. Chaotic and loud, to say the least!

Julie didn't even mind saying goodbye to Vonda when she left this time. Perhaps it was her friend's promise to come out and spend the Christmas holidays in Idaho. Or perhaps it was because she had something, or rather someone, to look forward to here.

Chip dropped her off outside the apartments, then rumbled back onto the road to meet his little family in Malad where they were visiting. Julie shouldered her bags and headed to her apartment, stopping at the mailbox on her way. Among the usual assortment of correspondence was a plain envelope, bearing only her name in Debbie's handwriting.

Julie tore it open, then noticed the curtains at Mrs. Ellsberg's window move aside. Obviously, some things hadn't changed in her absence, she thought sourly as she went inside to read the letter. It wasn't good news. Mrs. Ellsberg had found out about their cats!

Apparently a babysitter didn't know the rules and let them out to play in the sandbox when she was tending. The landlady was fit to be tied, lifting them by the tails and throwing them into a box until Debbie could return. Cody cried and cried. When Debbie unwittingly mentioned Julie's name in her hasty excuse, Mrs. Ellsberg hit the roof.

". . . So I'll be finding a new place to rent by the end of the month," Debbie wrote at the end of her note, "but I'm not sure what she has planned for you. She wouldn't say. Anyway, the cats are safe with me at my mom's for now. Sorry about this, and good luck with you-know-who!"

Julie glanced through the rest of her mail. An official-looking letter lurked at the bottom of the pile. She ripped it open, and as suspected, it was an eviction notice served on the grounds of non-payment of rent. That's right, September's rent! In her rush, she'd totally forgotten it.

Oh, well. Julie wasn't upset. She had half a notion to start packing. There was something she needed to do first, though. After quickly washing off the city's grime and slipping into fresh clothes, she grabbed a crumbled piece of pottery from the discard heap and dashed out the front door.

Mrs. Ellsberg stopped her before she could close it. "Young lady, I am so upset by what has happened this week."

"I know, I know," Julie said impatiently, bypassing the older woman and heading for her car.

Mrs. Ellsberg was not to be denied her rage. "You've gone too far this time!"

"I know!" Julie stopped, exasperated. "But it wasn't Debbie's fault, so please let her stay."

"Certainly not!" the landlady huffed. "Not after what she said. Imagine telling me to go to. . . ."

When Mrs. Ellsberg threw a hand to her chest with dramatic flair, Julie couldn't resist saying, "Why I can imagine that, rather vividly in fact. Now I've got to go!"

After a quick drive through Birch Creek, Julie didn't see Mark's Jeep at either Jackson Acres or the West farm. She stopped on her way back down the highway to see if Sarah knew his whereabouts. Her response completely shocked Julie. Maybe there was hope after all!

"He left about an hour ago." Sarah was anxious to thwart the latest of Mark's wild schemes. "We've got to stop him before he does something foolish."

"I agree," Julie replied, referring to the fact that Mark had to be stopped. She didn't exactly think his idea was foolish. Actually, it was quite romantic. But time was running short.

"Maybe you can catch him at Grandma Parsons'," Sarah called out as Julie dashed to her car. "Let's hope she's in a talkative mood."

Julie felt another surge of hope. When wasn't Mrs. Parsons in a talkative mood? Even so, she had no problem driving the speed limit as she rushed to Logan. She just had to catch Mark.

There were so many things she had to tell him . . . like she loved him and accepted him no matter what. She wanted to get the explanations and apologies over with quickly. She wanted to sit in the porch swing with him. She wanted to spend the rest of her life in his arms.

Oh, please, please, she prayed, let her find him soon. Before it was too late. She couldn't possibly endure another flight to New York tonight, could she? Well, she could if she had no other choice. But please . . .

As Julie pulled onto Mrs. Parsons' street, she knew her prayers were answered. Mark's Jeep was idling at the curb. There was a big suitcase in the back. He really was serious. Thank goodness she'd made it in time.

Julie skidded to a stop, jumped from the car, and ran into the house before her quick knock could be answered. Mrs. Parsons was sitting at the bottom of the long staircase, stroking her cat on the head. Mark was nowhere in sight.

"Why, Julie!" Mrs. Parsons said with a start, "I thought you were in New York."

"I was," Julie explained breathlessly, "but I'm back. Where's Mark?"

Mrs. Parsons nodded discreetly towards the bathroom door at the top of the stairs. "He should be done in a minute."

Just then the bathroom door opened, and Mark bounded down the stairs two at a time. Julie wanted to cry for happiness at the sight of the man she loved. He was dressed in jeans and a polo shirt with his new cowboy boots polished to a shine. She never remembered him looking so good.

"Guess I'm about ready to go, Gran . . ."

Mark froze when he saw Julie. He was speechless. Was this another dream? If so, he never wanted to wake up. He reached out and touched her just to see if she was real. She was!

They rushed into each other's arms, warmed by the love and

acceptance they found there. For the longest time, neither moved or spoke. And for the first time in decades, Mrs. Parsons couldn't think of a thing to say, so she quietly slipped outside.

Finally they stirred from the heavenly hug. "You're supposed to be in New York." Mark's statement sounded more like a question.

"I just got back today," Julie said. "Boy, that old Pine Valley landscape never looked so good."

"It did?" Mark looked at her intently. "You're glad to be back?"

"Of course! I couldn't wait to. . . ." Julie began, then saw the relieved, yet anguished look on his face. It suddenly struck her. "Oh, no! You didn't think I'd gone back to the city for good, did you?"

"Well, it wouldn't be the first time I'd lost out to glamour and glitz." He tried to sound nonchalant.

Julie wasn't fooled. "Oh, Mark! I love it here, I promise. I wouldn't have gone to New York at all, but Vonda needed me. She went into a diabetic coma, and I rushed back to be with her. I tried calling you before I left."

"I was gone." Mark paused. "So is Vonda all right?"

"She's recovering nicely, thank you." Julie was touched by his concern. "Where were you all week anyway?"

"All week? You called me more than once?"

"The operators all know me by name now."

"I was in Boise for some teachers' meetings. While I was there . . ." He stopped. Julie was squatting down, rummaging through a huge purse. He stared at her with a curious expression. "Looking for something?"

"Yeah," she pulled out a misshapen piece of pottery, "this. This was supposed to be your birthday present, this and about a dozen others like it. I was trying to put the shape of Angel's Peak into the pattern, but it just wouldn't turn out right."

It certainly didn't look right. The blob of dark brown that Julie pointed to reminded Mark of a two-humped camel. He grinned at her. "I see."

"I didn't really want to get you those scriptures. It wasn't my intention to put any undue pressure on you. But they seemed to call to me from the window of the bookstore. I tried to resist, but after a quick prayer, I knew that I had to buy them."

"The Lord must have really wanted me to get my hands on them then," he replied in an even tone.

Julie was relieved. She half-feared that he would stomp out again if she even mentioned them. In a rush, she continued, "I realized something in New York, Mark. I love you. And I'm willing to accept you just the way you are. Church or not, I'll love you forever."

"Oh, Julie!" Mark buried his face in her sweet-smelling hair.

"I'll never mention the Church again," she promised after a moment of relishing in his embrace, "and I'm going to return those books as soon as . . ."

"You can't."

"That's right," Julie lamented. "Your name's engraved on them, and I wrote inside. Well, we'll just have to hide them. . . ."

"Don't you dare hide my scriptures," Mark said with an indignant grin. "How could I take them to church with me if you did that?"

She looked puzzled. "What?"

"Julie," his tone was serious, "while I was alone in the motel in Boise, I decided to prove you wrong—to read the scriptures and try that prayer thing. When it didn't work, I'd tell you all to leave me alone about it once and for all. My plan, uh, backfired."

"Because it worked?" Julie asked quietly, hopefully.

"It sure did. I can't really explain how I know, but I know that the Book of Mormon is true. Weird, huh?"

"No." Her voice had a reverent tone. "Wonderful!"

"You were right about a lot of things, Julie. I blamed the Church, I think, when I was really feeling guilty. I feel a lot different about the Church now. Oh, I'm not one hundred percent yet. It will take time to get back into the swing of things, but I'm willing to try."

"I can't ask for any more than that."

After another long, and very satisfying hug, Mark said, in a low, husky voice, "We're meant to be together, Julie. It was planned in heaven by the angels, I think."

"What makes you say that?"

"Promise you won't laugh," he insisted. She shook her head, so he continued. "I think I've had one of those life-after-death experiences."

"This week?"

"No, back when I had my surgery, but I just remembered it today in a dream. Maybe it was just a dream, I don't know."

"Can you tell me about it? I mean, if it's too sacred or something, I'll understand."

"It was special, but I'd like to share it with you. Come on, let's sit down." Once they were settled on the sofa in the parlor, he began. "You know how I couldn't remember anything about that day?"

When Julie nodded, he went on, "Well, in my dream, I remembered all of it . . . calling you, falling down on the lawn, old Max howling for Ma. I remember going to the emergency room and even being in the recovery room after the surgery. You were there, Julie, with some pink thing hanging out the back of your sweats."

"That was my pajamas," Julie felt goosebumps rising on her arms, "but I didn't mention that to you. It was kind of embarrassing."

"Hmm," Mark felt a strange prickling under his skin, too. Was it the Spirit telling him that this was much more than a dream? "Anyway, you were shaking me and yelling."

"I was telling you to breathe."

"But it felt so good not to. I was kind of floating over my body, and then I saw a light in the corner of the room. I went up there, and it was a long, green tunnel. It's almost like I was pulled inside. Pretty soon it was like a quiet lane with trees on either side.

"I came to a fork in the path and had to make a decision. On one side, I could see Angel's Peak, on the other, mountains too majestic to describe. On the trail by those mountains were people dressed in white—Pa, Grandpa Jackson, Grandpa and Grandma West, and little Sadie, looking cute as ever.

"What was to decide? I almost ran straight over to her. Then I paused to see who was on the other trail, the one by Angel's Peak. It was you, Julie, holding your arms out to me so invitingly. I knew I had to decide between life with you or eternity with Sadie."

"And you came back to me," Julie stated quietly.

"I sure did." Mark kissed her nose.

"When you woke up from the anesthesia, you must have been telling Sadie that you were sorry to leave her," Julie's voice quivered. "Oh, Mark, what a horrid choice for you to be faced with."

"I don't regret my decision a minute. It's like I finally had some closure with Sadie. And I know that she'll be there when the time comes. But for now, it's time for this . . ."

He leaned toward her. She leaned toward him. In a breath of time, their lips melted together. A rapturous tingle spread down to Julie's toes. Mark could not get enough of her sweet taste. The world ceased to exist. An eternity later, they parted lips, but held each other tight.

Mark said, "Now do you see why I had to find you, no matter what?"

"I see." Julie's voice was husky. "Were you really going to New York?"

"You betcha!"

"And just how did you expect to find me there?" she asked with a grin.

"Start at Mercy Hospital," Mark shrugged, "but I'd have knocked on every door in the city, if necessary, until I found you."

"That's a lot of doors."

"Every one of them," he insisted.

"And what if I refused to come back?"

She was teasing now, but Mark wasn't. "I'd have boarded up the farmhouse, sold my Jeep, and sent my resume to any school out there that would take it."

She was touched. "You would be willing to stay in the city with me?"

"Yup!"

"Even in a skyscraper?"

"I would climb a rickety old ladder to the moon to be with you."

Julie didn't trust her voice as she realized the extent of the sacrifice he was willing to make for her. He hated cities, heights, and commitment, but he was willing to try all three for her. He really did love her.

"Now," he rose, then knelt on one knee and took her hands into his own, "let's make this official before I chicken out again. Julie, the love of my life, will you marry me?"

"Of course!" Julie felt tears of joy fall. "There is nothing in the world I would like better."

"Good, now let's seal that promise with another kiss."

"This could be addicting," she giggled.

"I hope so."

"We need to talk about living arrangements," Julie announced later.

They were sitting in the porch swing, watching the last rays of sunset fade into a gentle lavender glow. They had slipped away from Logan, coming to this private paradise in the shadow of Angel's Peak as quickly as possible. There would be time enough for sharing their news tomorrow.

"After all our work, don't tell me you don't want to live here now!"

"Far from it!" Julie looked back at the farmhouse behind them. "I fell in love with this house the minute I saw it."

"Before or after you fell in love with me?"

"Hmm, let's see . . . ," Julie teased. "Seriously, I'm on the brink of joining the world's homeless population." She explained the incident with Mrs. Ellsberg and the cats.

Mark had a ready solution. "Well, why don't you and Uncle Sam move in here then? The house is ready."

"But what about you? Are you sure you wouldn't mind?"

"Under the circumstances, I'd mind more if you had to live by Old Chicken-Snoop any longer."

"Old Chicken-Snoop?"

Mark smiled sheepishly. "We used to call Mrs. Ellsberg that in grade school. Anyway, is tomorrow soon enough for us to move you up?"

"Perfect! And I really don't have that much stuff."

"Not that much stuff? I've lifted that crazy potter's wheel of yours. It gave me an attack of appendicitis."

"Very funny," Julie punched him on the arm. "Now about your house on Jackson Acres. . . ."

"You have plans for that, too?"

"As a matter of fact, I do. Debbie and Chip will be needing a new place to live soon, too. Do you think they could rent it?"

"I don't know why not. I'll just bunk at Ma's until I can join you up here. Hey, Julie, exactly when were you baptized?"

"First part of October. Why?"

"I just wondered how long I'd have to wait until I can take you upstairs and really let you know how much I love you."

That thought appealed to Julie. "We could get married tomorrow if you want."

It took a great deal of self-control for Mark not to agree. "I suppose we could, but not if we get married in the temple."

"Really?" She turned to look at him, wondering if he was serious. She had only hoped that someday they would go to the temple. She never dreamed it would be this soon.

"I plan on doing it right this time," Mark avowed as he nibbled on her fingertips. "This marriage is going to last a lifetime and beyond."

Chapter Twenty

Mark offered to wash the dishes while Julie went upstairs to change before they left for Logan. Glancing at the hefty stack of dirty pots and pans in the sink, Julie quickly agreed. *Six weeks of marriage and he's still so good to me,* she thought with amazement as she dashed up the stairs.

"Be ready in half an hour?" Mark called after her retreating figure.

"No problem!"

In their bedroom, Julie removed her dress. Surveying the marks of a dozen tiny fingerprints, she decided it wasn't beyond repair. Since she and Mark had been called as nursery leaders, Julie had yet to leave the Birch Creek meetinghouse unscathed.

Maybe it would help, Mark told her often, if she didn't get down on her hands and knees to crawl around with the kids. Julie couldn't help it. They were so darling. She couldn't wait to start a family of her own. Mark readily agreed.

Julie patted her stomach and wondered. If the miracle of conception hadn't occurred yet, it wasn't for a lack of trying, she thought with a smile at the rumpled bedsheets. The days since their wedding were full of laughter and happiness, but their nights were full of fire!

Julie hurriedly dressed, combed her hair, and freshened her lipstick before joining Mark in the kitchen again. The sink was empty, except for a large pot with a thick, black crust stuck to the bottom of it. It was half full of soapy water.

"Pretty bad, huh?" Julie asked, poking a finger at the stubborn mess.

She had tried making soup yesterday, then got involved with helping Mark dismantle an old shed outside. By the time she returned to the kitchen, the soup was ruined. They ate frozen dinners from a ready supply in a freezer on the back porch.

"It just needs to soak a little," Mark assured her as he placed a stack of plates into the cupboard. "We'll do better next time."

Julie sighed. Though Mark was very tolerant of her kitchen skills, or rather lack of skills, they were both getting tired of spaghetti. And yet, every time she tried something new, it was a disaster. He never complained about the things she set before him, but even she had taste buds.

Julie sighed, "Maybe you'd have been better off marrying LuAnn Frost after all."

"LuAnn Frost?!" Mark scowled. "Why in the hell . . . oh, excuse me . . . heck would I want to marry her?"

"Because she can cook," Julie answered glumly.

"Well, I happen to be in love with you, Julie dearest."

"Love doesn't fill your stomach."

"But it sure makes eating some of the things we cook a lot easier," he laughed. "Besides, eating frozen dinners across the table from you beats eating filet mignon alone any day. Hey, weren't Thad and Cody cute in sacrament meeting today?"

"They sure were," Julie agreed, remembering how they took the closing song into their own hands. Since moving up to Jackson Acres, Cody idolized Thad, and the two had become best of friends. What trouble one didn't think of getting into, the other one soon did. "Do you think our children will be that naughty at church?"

"Plan on it," Mark said knowingly. "You'll want to take their temperatures if they ever sit quietly through a whole meeting. Are you ready to go?"

"Sure, let me just turn off the stereo."

Julie paused a minute in the family room and looked around.

The whole house was really taking shape. Coming up from behind, Mark embraced her, and resting his chin upon her head, said, "Not a bad-looking home, Mrs. Jackson. You've done a good job on it."

"We both have," Julie agreed. "And I must admit it's a good thing you were in love with Jackie Carter when you were ten."

"And why is that?"

"Because if it had been any other initials," Julie pointed to a roughly-carved heart, encasing a jagged, but rather fitting "MJ + JC" on the side of the bannister in the hallway, "you'd have had a time sanding that thing off."

"Well, bless old Jackie's heart then," Mark grinned and was quickly jabbed in the ribs with an elbow. "Let's get out of here before you find any more reasons to cause me bodily harm. Want me to get the Jello?"

"Sure," she replied as she checked to see the front door was locked.

"You know, Julie," Mark remarked as they walked out to the Explorer, "this doesn't look half bad."

"Well, you can't do much to ruin Jello," she said with a smug grin.

"I don't know about that," Mark joked. Julie wanted to punch him in the ribs again, but she wouldn't take the risk of harming her wiggly red creation. She even buckled a seat belt around it in the backseat of the car. Then waving goodbye to Max and Uncle Sam on the back porch, they were off.

Julie smiled as they pulled away from the house with its trimmed yard. The huge pile of rubbish from fixing up the house was gone. The gardens were tilled, and the rose bushes fertilized with fresh manure. Even the autumn leaves had been raked and burned.

The farmyard also looked good. The corral was finished, the barn was painted, and only the sturdiest sheds and outbuildings remained. The first two of what they hoped would be a long line of fine horses grazed in a nearby padlock.

As a wedding gift, Mark had planned to give Julie the mare named Little Al. Julie wanted to do the same with Mark's favorite mount. They both went to great lengths to keep their plans a secret. Rick had his hands full with that, but the double surprise was a big success.

They talked about it again as they drove to Oakwood. Julie scarcely noticed passing Casa Grande Apartments, except to wonder what Mrs. Ellsberg was gossiping about now. She was sure the old snoop had found something, whether it was true or not.

"You know," Julie laughed as they passed the tall Pine Valley Grain Grower's towers on the southern edge of town, "when I first came here last spring, I thought those looked like miniature skyscrapers."

"What a city girl!" Mark moaned, but it sounded like an endearment.

After making a dozen trips with Mark hauling wheat for Steve, she knew what the once mysterious buildings were. Even now, a shifting stream of golden grain was being loaded onto railroad cars headed for mills, then bakeries, then markets, then her toaster. And people thought the cities were the only places where important things happened.

Before long, they left the peacefulness of Pine Valley. In the canyon beyond, Julie thought how drab the hillsides looked in November's gray. The last time she had been through there, six weeks earlier, it had been alive with the vibrant colors of fall.

But then, Mark and Julie weren't looking at the scenery much on that trek. They were too wrapped up in each other as they drove to the temple in Logan to be wed for time and all eternity. And during their honeymoon through the Yellowstone area, they rarely looked at the scenery at all.

Finally, they pulled up in front of Grandma Parsons' home. Actually, it was more like down the block as they weren't the first ones to arrive. Although it was the week before Thanksgiving, a hearty feast of turkey and fixings sat upon the table as loved ones gathered around for a farewell party.

"Oh no," Grandma Parsons shook her fork vigorously at one point during the meal, "I couldn't possibly wait until after Christmas to go. I have to get to St. George as soon as possible. If I don't hurry, Gladys Welker may get her hands on Fred Shaw after all. She was trying her darnedest last spring, but I held on until she went back to her summer home in Montana. But I've heard that she is on the move, and I don't have a minute to lose. It's not easy keeping widows away from eligible men down there, you know."

"Fred Shaw, huh?" Mark teased his grandmother. "Don't tell me you're going to come back as Grandma Shaw next year."

"I just might at that," she answered with a wink, "if old Fred's heart keeps beatin' that long."

Once the meal was over, the men retired to watch a football game while the women chattered in the kitchen and the children romped in the basement. When she'd cleared her share of the dishes from the table, Julie excused herself. She stepped quietly out onto the front porch.

It was mild and warm for November, but she shivered a little as she gazed up at the beauty of the temple on the hill. She couldn't quite believe that she and Mark had been there. The thick gold band and sparkling diamond on her finger said it was true. So did the new wedding portrait on Mrs. Parsons' wall. Julie sighed with happiness.

She heard the door behind her open and shut, then Mark gently put his arms around her from behind. "Finally getting your fill of all this big family stuff?"

"Never." Julie relaxed her head against his chest. "I've always wanted a big family, and I can't thank you enough for every one of them."

"Even Aunt Vergie?"

"Even her. You don't know how good it feels to belong somewhere after being alone all these years."

"You'll always belong right here, Julie. And with this bunch, you'll never have to worry about being alone again, believe me. By the way, is your friend Vonda still coming out for Christmas?"

"Yeah, she called yesterday and said everything was arranged. Are you sure you don't mind?"

"I can't wait to meet her," Mark avowed with a kiss. "What else did she have to say?"

"Oh, she just told me again how sorry she was that she couldn't come for the wedding. She's still mad at her doctors for not letting her travel that far yet. She said, 'You have insulin in Idaho, too, don't you, child?!' I assured her that we most certainly do."

"Speaking of that," Mark laughed, "I think Aunt Stella was pleasantly surprised to find anything of a civilized nature out here. I suspect she liked it more than she'd ever admit."

"I think you're right," Julie smiled, remembering Stella's visit.

Julie wasn't surprised when her aunt insisted upon providing a dress for the wedding. She even sent her aunt a diagram of the necessary modesty requirements for the temple. Stella called weekly with reports on the progress of the designer gown. Same old Stella.

Julie was very surprised, however, when her aunt called from the Salt Lake airport about a week before the wedding. She had decided to deliver the dress by hand and was fuming. Imagine, no taxicabs there would take her to Idaho! Julie quickly drove down and retrieved her.

As they drove northward, Stella couldn't get over the scenery. And once they arrived, she was quite taken with the handsome farmer Julie planned to wed. She even allowed him, in his simple, respectful way, to call her Aunt Stella. Now that was something!

The wedding gown fit perfectly. Stella had even been quite understanding about not being able to see Julie wear it inside the temple. She insisted upon paying for a lavish wedding breakfast afterwards, though, and decorated the West farmhouse extravagantly for the small, simple open house held there that evening.

Only one thing seemed to irritate Stella. Mark and Julie wanted to leave right behind their last guest. After all, there were dishes to wash, a number of helpers to thank, presents to open. When Julie whispered in her aunt's ear the exact reason why they were in such a hurry, Stella actually blushed. She didn't think anyone still waited until the wedding night!

Before they could go, though, Stella extracted three promises from Mark. The first was to take good care of Julie. The second was to allow Stella to send out little things from New York to help them decorate their house. And the third promise was. . . .

Mark broke into her thoughts. "You think your aunt will really hold me to that promise about bringing you back to New York often to visit?"

"You can count on it," Julie chuckled.

"I was afraid of that," Mark groaned. After contemplating his sad fate for a minute, he remarked, "Hey, did I tell you I talked to the bishop today about getting little Sadie sealed to us?"

"You did?!" Julie asked excitedly. They had both agreed to wait until after the rush of the wedding to check into that possibility. And to Julie's surprise, Mark was even willing to try and find Denise, if necessary, for the ordinance to be valid and binding. "What did he say?"

"Well, he wasn't too sure about the exact procedure, but he'll check and get back with us. He gave me a form for you to fill out to have your parents' temple work done, too."

After a few sniffles, Julie gazed up at the temple. "Isn't it beautiful?" she whispered.

"You sure are."

"I'm serious! The blessings of the temple are endless. We've been sealed forever, and now my parents can have the same opportunity, and so on, and so on. I can't even explain the joy that brings to me. Our Savior must have really loved us to make all of this possible."

Mark agreed. "Looking at you across that altar was one of the most beautiful, touching things I've ever experienced. Even my memories of Sadie, dear as they are, don't touch my heart like you do, Julie."

"Oh, Mark," she sighed contentedly, "how can two people be as lucky as we are?"

"It's more than luck. We've been blessed. Hey, did I ever tell you I figured out what that unofficial 'mission' of yours was all about, Mrs. Jackson?"

"No, what?" she asked dreamily.

"This," he answered with feeling, "to love and be loved. To give me happiness and to let me give you happiness."

"And for that," Julie teased, "I was sent to the ends of the earth?"

"The angels must have known that they'd have a heck of a time getting me out to New York City to find you," Mark countered.

"That's true," Julie laughed. "That would have taken a miracle!"

Mark tightened his embrace. "Yeah? Well, you performed a miracle of sorts right here."

"It certainly was worth all my trouble then."

He laughed, then they fell into a comfortable silence, each reflecting on the extent of their blessings. After a few more minutes, Mark pulled away and said, "I think I'll go in and see if there is any more of your Jello left. It really was good."

"Really?"

"You bet. We just might make a cook out of you yet." He offered her his arm. "Care to join me?"

She declined, "Go ahead. I'll come in a few minutes."

Once she was alone, Julie silently thanked the Lord for all her blessings: a big family, a beautiful home, wonderful friends, a career she loved, and the very best husband in the whole world! Then she went inside. She had to make sure Mark wasn't really feeding her Jello to Grandma Parsons' cat!

ABOUT THE AUTHOR

A woman of many interests and talents, Janet Bergera is a busy mother who also works as a registered nurse and pursues such varied hobbies as interior decorating, making handicrafts, reading, star-gazing, and watching St. Louis Cardinal baseball. *Vital Signs* is her first novel, although she has enjoyed writing from an early age.

Janet, her husband, Scott, and their four children live in Utah Valley.